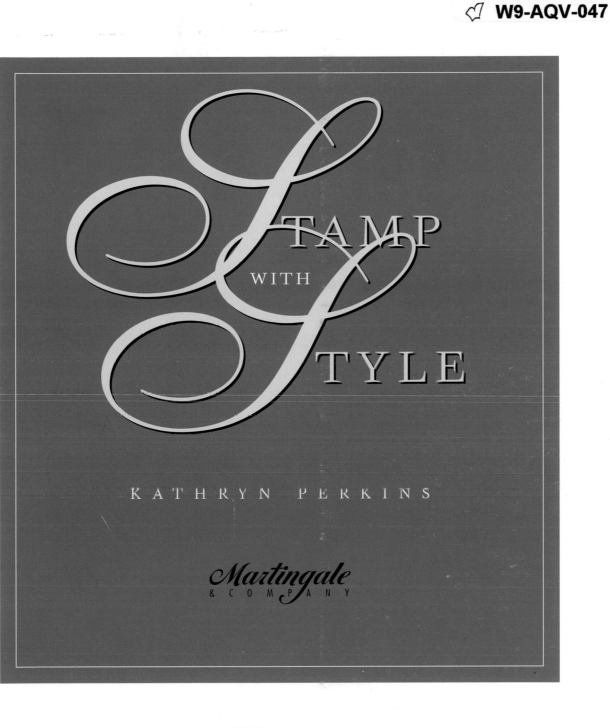

Stamp

WITH

Style

KATHRYN PERKINS

Martingale
& COMPANY

Acknowledgments

Many thanks to my family for their undying support and to my business partner,
Ann Zazzi, for her constant encouragement.

Stamp with Style
More than 50 Creative Cards and Projects

Text © 1998 by Kathryn Perkins
Illustrations and Photographs © 1998 Martingale & Company
All rubber stamps used in this book have trademark registration with the U.S. Copyright Office. The author gratefully acknowledges the following for their permission to use rubber stamp images not created by Impress Stamps: All Night Media (© Michel & Company, made under license by All Night Media, Inc.), Co-Motion, Darcie's Country Folk (© Darcie Heater), DeNami Design, Dottie's Darlings, Ducks in a Row (© Joan Farber), Fred B. Mullett, Good Stamps Stamp Goods, Graven Images, Hero Arts Rubber Stamps, Inc., Hot Potatoes, Imaginations Inc., Impress Rubber Stamps, Inkadinkadoo, Lasting Impressions, Leavenworth Jackson, Magenta, Mail Expressions, Marks of Distinction, Mostly Animals (copyrighted artwork reproduced under license), Personal Stamp Exchange, Picture Show, Portfolio Rubber Stamps, Posh Impressions, Printworks (© Annette Allen Watkins), Renaissance Rubber Stamp Co., Rubber Stampede, Rubber Stamps of America, Stamp Francisco, Stamps by Judith, Stampendous Inc. Rubber Stamps, TooMuchFun Rubber Stamps, Uptown Rubber Stamps.

MARTINGALE & COMPANY
20205 144th Avenue NE
Woodinville, WA 98072-8478 USA

Martingale
& COMPANY

Printed in Hong Kong   03 02   8 7 6 5

Library of Congress Cataloging-in-Publication Data
Perkins, Kathryn
    Stamp with style : more than 50 creative cards and projects /
  Kathryn Perkins.
        p.   cm.
    ISBN 1-56477-224-1
    1. Rubber stamp printing.   2. Greeting cards.   I. Title
  TT867.P46 1998
  761—DC21   98-7869
                                                                          CIP

Credits
Editing, Design, and Production: Watershed Books
Illustration: Laurel Strand
Photography: Brent Kane

Contents

Introduction 4
DESIGNING 4
  Color 5
  Scale and Proportion 5
  Composition 5
TECHNIQUES 5
  Stamping 5
  Heat Embossing 5
  Pressure Embossing 6
  Folding 6
  Masking 6
  Photo Transfer 6
TOOLS AND SUPPLIES 7
  Ink Pads 7
  Pens and Markers 7
  Colored Pencils 7
  Paper 7
  Adhesives 8
  Creative Fasteners 8
  Text Composition Tools 9
  Cutting Tools 9
  Basic Tools and Supplies 9
GETTING ORGANIZED 9
  Greeting Card Keepsake Book 10

January 12
  Leaf Thank You Note 14
  Embossed Flower Card 15
  Thank You Fold Note 16
  Congratulations Card 17

February 18
  Beaded Valentine 20
  Chocolate Valentine 22
  Accordion Photo Valentine 23

March 24
  Balloon in a Slide Frame Card 26
  Birthday Boy Card 27
  Fiftieth Birthday Card 28
  Birthday Present Card 29
  Package Birthday Invitation 30

April 32
  Ribbon Rose Card 34
  Checkered Flowers Thank You Card 35
  Carrots in a Pot Card 36
  Handmade Gift Bag 38
  Birdhouse Gift Tag 40

May 42
  Alphabet Bead Baby Card 44
  Baby Shower Invitation 45
  Woven Ribbon Card 46
  Baby Shower Favor Package 47

June 48
  Romantic Wedding Card 50
  Bridal Shower Invitation 51
  Angel Wedding Card 52
  Father's Day Card 53
  Wedding Invitation & Reception Card 54

July 56
  Summer Note Cards 58
  Note Card Packet 59

August 60
  Bee Card 62
  Bee Book Cover 63
  Pivoting Sunshine Card 64
  Bee Pillow 66
  Paper Coasters & Take-Out Boxes 67

September 68
  Cutaway Tulip Card 70
  Floral Vellum Card with Beads 71
  Pressed Flower Gift Tag 72
  Floral Fold Note 73

October 74
  Trick-or-Treat Pack 76
  Jack-O'-Lantern Photo Card 77
  Halloween Party Invitation 78
  Escaping Ghost Card 79

November 80
  Cocktail Party Invitation 82
  Square Photo Invitation 83
  Book-Style Invitation 84
  Explosive New Year's Eve Invitation 86

December 88
  Photo Holiday Greeting Card 90
  Christmas Gift Bag & Tree Ornament 91
  Christmas Greeting Card 92
  Holiday Paper Mitten 93
  Spiral Christmas Tree Card 94

INDEX 95
SOURCES 96

Introduction

Creating fine handmade cards using rubber stamps is a versatile and satisfying art form. One of my favorite things about collecting rubber stamps and creating stamp art is that it is an art of sharing. You get to keep the stamps, yet share your visual interpretation of feelings and sentiments tailored for a specific person or a special occasion. I am continually amazed when I visit a friend's home and find a card I've sent prominently displayed. In this day of e-mail, faxes, and cell phones, your handmade card will be treasured for the thoughtfulness that went into it, as well as its beauty.

You can enjoy rubber stamping in its simplest form—with a rubber stamp, ink, and a piece of paper—or embellish your stamped image with techniques that add depth and texture in combination with different colored inks, papers, and decorative elements. I hope this book will enhance your rubber stamping projects and will inspire you to explore some new techniques. Don't feel confined to the designs and methods in this book, however. Look around for new accessories and experiment with new tools and techniques. That's how someone turned a tube squeezer into a paper crimper, and a heat gun became an embossing tool.

Once you learn to make the many cards and projects in this book, use your newly gained knowledge, skills, and confidence to design your own cards. Your own inspiration is the most stimulating aspect of any art or craft. What inspires me may be a color combination or simply a feeling that I want to convey. I'm always alert to new sources of inspiration—the

color of a coat on someone rushing past me in the mall, dishes in a store window, colors in my neighbor's garden, or an advertisement in a magazine. Of course, you can also use your local rubber stamp store for card ideas, as well as the many rubber stamping publications on the market. When you keep your eyes and mind open to the little inspirations around you every day, you may be surprised at what you see!

Finally, be sure to finish every project you create by signing it. There are many *Hand stamped by* stamps at your local rubber stamp store, or you may wish to design your own. Choose a tiny stamp that you love and develop a distinctive signature to identify your artwork. When your friends receive the cards you've crafted, they will be delighted to see your signature on the back.

Designing

Designing, to me, is the most enjoyable and satisfying aspect of creating cards and gifts using rubber stamps. The principles and elements of design that apply to any visual art form also apply to rubber stamped cards and projects, but you needn't be schooled in design to create beautiful cards. I suggest that you simply examine card compositions that you find appealing. What is it that you like about a card? It will become apparent that the artist who created the cards you like applied the principles and elements of good design. Here are some guidelines most relevant to the rubber stamp projects in this book.

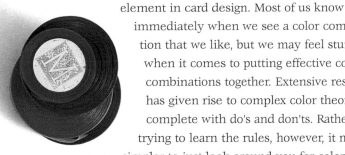

COLOR—Color is probably the most apparent element in card design. Most of us know immediately when we see a color combination that we like, but we may feel stumped when it comes to putting effective color combinations together. Extensive research has given rise to complex color theories, complete with do's and don'ts. Rather than trying to learn the rules, however, it may be simpler to just look around you for color combinations to imitate. Mother Nature frivolously mixes colors of various hues and intensities, creating stunning combinations that may defy the rules. Your own personal preference may take precedence when you select colors for your cards and projects, and patient experimentation will yield the best results.

SCALE AND PROPORTION—Scale and proportion are design elements that may be most troublesome for beginning stampers. Because most rubber stamp images are relatively small, a single stamp on the front of a card can appear lost. To bring the scale of the card down to a size that is appropriate for the stamped image, frame the design. Either draw a border around the design using a pen and straight edge or cut out the design and layer contrasting colors of paper beneath it.

COMPOSITION—Once you have envisioned your project, begin by stamping the images on scrap paper cut the same size as your card. You may prefer to stamp all the designs on scrap paper and cut out each one, then move each piece independently. Sometimes the card will come together easily except for a single element, such as the color of a stamped image. Stamp the design on scrap paper in several colors, cut them out, and place each one on the card to decide what looks best.

Techniques

Rubber stamping may not be rocket science, but knowledge of a few simple paper-craft techniques will give you the tricks of the trade you need to make polished, professional-looking cards and expand your design options. As with any art or craft, practicing different techniques will give you the skills you need to achieve satisfactory results, so be sure to try these techniques on scrap paper first.

STAMPING—The rubber stamps that make the best impressions are wood-mounted stamps with red or gray rubber dies, neatly trimmed and mounted on a fairly thick foam rubber cushion. Rubber stamps are generally trimmed and assembled by hand, so each one may vary slightly. One stamp may need only light pressure when inking, while another may need to be rocked in a particular direction to get a complete imprint. Foam-backed stamps like the ones sold in many sets are trickier to work with because the backing is not as hard as the wood-backed stamps.

Ink your stamp by dabbing it on the pad several times, then press the stamp on paper, applying even pressure. Check your stamped image. If parts of the image are missing, be sure to thoroughly re-ink and apply a little more pressure to the missing area on the next stamping.

If you get an unwanted ink blob, clean the stamp die thoroughly with a wet paper towel, then re-ink and press firmly, but not too hard, and without rocking the stamp. Be sure to continually wipe your stamping surface and keep your hands clean—I've ruined many a project by touching the paper with an inky finger.

Placing a smooth, clean, flat surface beneath your stamping paper will help you make a precise image. A slight bit of padding, such as a magazine or plastic cutting board, makes for nice, crisp impressions.

HEAT EMBOSSING—Heat embossing, or thermography, is a way to achieve raised relief in an image. To create a heat-embossed image, ink the stamp with a slow-drying ink such as a pigment or special embossing ink, a slightly tacky ink available either clear or tinted. Once the image is stamped, sprinkle it with embossing powder; it will stick to the wet or tacky ink. Tap the excess powder onto a piece of paper and return it to the container.

The next step is to heat the embossing powder, which will melt in seconds to create a raised, glossy design. A heat gun is the preferred tool for this step, but you can also use an electric stove element, an iron, or a toaster oven. A heat gun is a hand-held electric tool that gently blows air just hot enough to melt embossing powder in about twenty to thirty seconds. Be sure to exercise caution with your heat source and never allow children to use it unsupervised.

Embossing powders are available in several varieties. I prefer clear embossing powder because it gives a vivid, enameled look over any color pigment ink. Ultra-thick embossing powder lays down a heavier layer of powder to give a more dimensional effect. Embossing powders are available in many colors and finishes, including glitter, sparkle, pearlized, iridescent, and gold-flecked. One jar will last a long time if you are careful to pour back all excess powder each time you use it.

If you use colored embossing powders, it is important to remove all the specks that may stick to the paper outside the image area. After pouring off the excess powder, tap the paper gently to remove the remaining specks. If there is any unwanted powder remaining on the paper, remove it with a watercolor brush.

PRESSURE EMBOSSING—Pressure embossing does not actually involve rubber stamps, but it may provide a nice complement to a stamped image. The effect is more subtle than stamping. The paper is actually raised where it has been pressed into the design.

To get this raised effect you will use a brass or plastic

HEAT EMBOSSING

template or stencil. It is usually necessary to have a light source behind the stencil. A light box is ideal, but if you don't have one you can tape the stencil to a window and let the natural daylight shine through. Place the paper face down over the stencil and run an embossing stylus along the inside of the stencil image, pressing steadily. The stylus will move more smoothly if you first rub the paper lightly with waxed paper.

FOLDING—Crisp folds are the hallmark of professional-looking handmade cards and papers. To get a smooth fold, first score the paper to crush the fibers. Measure and mark the fold line on each edge of the paper. Then connect the marks by running a scoring tool such as the sharp edge of a burnisher, an embossing stylus, or a bone folder along a ruler. Rub the fold with the smooth side of the burnisher.

MASKING—Masking is a way to add depth or perspective by creating a repeat or offset image. Begin by stamping the image that will be in the foreground. To make the mask, stamp the image on a piece of thin scrap paper or a stick-on note, which will hold the mask neatly in place. Next, trim around the image just inside the design outline. Lay the mask exactly over the first impression and repeat the stamping so that the new image just overlaps the masked one. Remove the mask and your image is finished.

PHOTO TRANSFER—Transferring a photo image onto another piece of paper is a simple process that provides a startling effect on place cards, gift tags, invitations, and many other paper projects. You can combine this technique with rubber stamps to frame a portrait or create a picture of someone popping out of a birthday present.

To transfer photographs, photocopy your picture (use the photo option on the copier if it has one). Next, place the photocopy face down on the paper you're transferring it to and rub firmly across the image with a colorless blender pen, then rub it again with a burnisher. Remove the photocopy and your transfer is complete.

Tools and Supplies

With growing interest in rubber stamp arts and crafts, new inks have been developed that enhance stamped images. There are inks with different properties available in a wide variety of colors, as well as colored pencils, pens, and markers. There are also new scissors and paper punches that have decorative edges, and tools that you may have at home, such as a computer or sewing machine, that you can use to make cards.

INK PADS—Ink pads for rubber stamping generally have a surface raised beyond the edge of the container so you can rub the pad over the rubber stamp. This allows you to ink a stamp that is larger than the size of the pad, or just ink part of a stamp to combine different colors. To clean your rubber stamps, use a wet paper towel or commercial stamp cleaner.

The three types of inks used on the cards in this book are dye inks, pigment inks, and permanent craft inks. Each type has different properties, although all are nontoxic, water based, and acid free.

Dye inks are fast-drying inks that deliver an intense color and don't bleed into the paper. These inks are not particularly good for heat embossing.

Pigment inks are more like paint than dye inks. They are not absorbed by the paper, but sit on the surface. These inks are slow drying, which is a good attribute for heat embossing but a drawback if you are making many cards because you have to spread them out to dry.

Permanent craft inks, such as Fabrico permanent inks, are marketed as craft inks because they work as well on wood, plastic, paper, and other surfaces as they do on fabric. Fabrico must be heat set to be permanent or washable. Use an iron to set the ink on fabric; use a heat gun to set it on other surfaces. This ink is slow drying, so it is excellent for heat embossing.

FOLDING

PENS AND MARKERS—Marvy Markers, Le Plumes, and Tombows are all pens with water-based inks that can be applied directly to a rubber stamp. Although it may take more time to ink stamps with pens, the advantage is that you can apply many colors to a single stamped image. Marker inks dry relatively slowly on a rubber stamp, so there is plenty of time to apply several colors and the ink will still be wet enough to transfer to paper. After you make the first impression, remoisturize the stamp with a puff of your breath to get another imprint or two without re-inking. Clean the stamps with a wet paper towel or stamp cleaner.

Colored markers and pens make exceptionally sharp and vivid impressions on coated papers, while uncoated paper may absorb the ink, yielding a slightly blurred image. You can also use markers and pens to color an image after it is stamped on paper.

COLORED PENCILS—I like the soft hues and shades you can achieve with colored pencils. You can vary the pressure to produce lighter or darker hues or blend them to create a new color. For best results, good-quality colored pencils, such Berol Prismacolor, are worth the money.

On a heat-embossed image, it may be difficult to color close to the raised lines with the hard tip of a colored pencil. I prefer to use watercolor pencils for these images because you can spread the color with a wet watercolor paintbrush. Color the design with the pencil or create a color palette on a separate piece of paper. Be sure to practice with these pencils because the color changes when you add water.

PAPER—Rubber stampers have an incredible array of beautiful papers to choose from. You can select a paper both for the artistic look you want and for the type of ink you use. Textured, loose, absorbent papers may cause wetter inks, like those in markers, to bleed; pigment inks hold the sharpest image on this type of paper. Shiny or very dense paper, such as chrome-coat, is less absorbent. and you can make a wonderful impression on this paper with dye inks or markers, while pigment ink will not dry on coated paper unless it is set with embossing powder.

I love to use vellum because of its wonderful translucency. It is available in several weights, with the lightest being most transparent. This paper is tricky to stamp because it is not absorbent and even dye ink takes a while to dry. But be patient: I've been able to get pigment ink to dry on vellum if it's not too inky, and you can use a heat gun to speed the drying time. Heat embossing also works well, and when you apply pressure embossing, the stylus leaves an interesting white mark that adds to the raised effect.

Most colored papers can be stamped with any of the inks I've described. Experimenting is the best way to find the most suitable ink for each paper because it is not always easy to predict how an ink color may be altered by the shade of the paper. I generally don't recommend that you use construction paper if you want colored paper, because it fades readily and can be easily bent. However, it is a good choice for children's projects because it is relatively inexpensive.

There are also many lovely textured and printed papers that are not suitable for stamping, but which make interesting background layers and collages. Some stores sell a variety of off-cuts of these papers in grab bags.

Finally, a word about the weights of paper that work best for making cards. Papers come in a range of weights, from light to heavy. Most crafts in this book require card stock, which is usually about an eighty-pound weight. A few projects call for text-weight paper, which varies slightly in weight

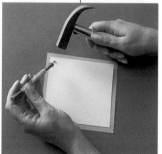

INSTALLING EYELET

but is comparable to a standard stationery paper.

ADHESIVES—Almost every project in this book requires gluing or taping at some stage, and the wrong adhesive can ruin a project. My favorite adhesive for most situations is rubber cement. It doesn't warp the paper, holds firmly, allows for repositioning, and cleans up easily. For large projects, I also like to use aerosol spray adhesive. Sprays can be messy, however, so be sure to protect the area around the paper you are spraying. I also use a glue stick for spot-gluing.

For many projects, adhesive tape works well. In addition to regular cellophane and invisible adhesive tapes, you can use double-sided tapes to adhere two papers together, although this tape is more expensive. When I want to achieve a raised effect, I use double-stick mounting foam.

These are only a few of the many adhesives on the market, and everyone seems to have a favorite. Experiment until you find one that works well for your project. Choose carefully because a good adhesive makes for a professional-looking card that holds together.

CREATIVE FASTENERS—Many of the projects in this book involve layering an array of papers. These layers can be attached to each other in many ways other than gluing. Eyelets or grommets can be used to bind a small booklet, attach two or more pieces of paper together, or create a pivoting effect. Eyelets require a special installation tool and a hammer. To install an eyelet, first punch a one-eighth-inch hole through all paper layers. Insert the eyelet, rolled edge down (preferably on a protected surface). Set the pointed tip of the eyelet tool in the open end of the eyelet and strike the opposite end gently with a hammer. To get a nice, rolled end, set an eyelet finishing tool over the end and again strike with a hammer.

Ribbons and decorative cords are another way to tie layers together. Another interesting technique is to sew your paper together using needle and thread or your sewing machine. When using a sewing machine, be sure to experiment with the thread tension to achieve an even stitch on the front.

TEXT COMPOSITION TOOLS—The style of typeface or writing used on a card lends as much to the overall design as the rubber stamp images and color. A computer may not sound like something you use for a rubber stamp project, but it is a very flexible tool for composing text. There are many beautiful computer fonts available that you can use to compose invitations or personal greetings. I love to try different fonts, sizes, and styles such as italic or bold. There is a large selection of fonts available; they can be purchased individually or as part of a large package.

I also encourage everyone to learn calligraphy and work to achieve a distinctive handwriting to give handwritten greetings a polished look.

CUTTING TOOLS—The first cutting tool you will want to own is a good quality paper cutter that is large enough to cut an 8½-by-11-inch sheet of paper. Next, buy a self-healing cutting mat. It makes an excellent surface for stamping as well as cutting. Many projects require an X-Acto knife, so get one or more of these knives and keep a supply of blades on hand. To make straight cuts with an X-Acto knife, use a metal ruler that has rubber or cork attached to the underside so it does not slip.

There is an enormous selection of scissors on the market equipped with decorative blades that cut shaped edges. I recommend the deckle-edge and scallop-edge scissors. Rotary cutters also come in a variety of shapes, including perforated. Hole punches, too, come in different sizes and shapes, from bicycles to Mickey Mouse. For a basic circle hole, purchase a size that fits the ribbon or eyelet you plan to feed

through it. You can also use a simple belt punch, which allows you to punch a hole in the middle of a card.

BASIC TOOLS AND SUPPLIES—These are the basic tools and supplies you will need for most projects in this book. Other tools and materials required for specific cards are listed in the project's materials list or in the directions.

- ✦ Paper cutter—to make straight and square cuts
- ✦ Straight edge or ruler—to measure and use as a guide for a knife or burnisher
- ✦ X-Acto knife—to make exact cuts and interior slits
- ✦ Cutting mat—to make accurate cuts with your X-Acto knife or rotary cutter
- ✦ Rubber cement—to glue paper to paper
- ✦ Burnisher—to score and crease paper
- ✦ Hole punch—to make ribbon holes

Getting Organized

Like many people, I often regret that I failed to budget time to execute the card I had in mind for a special occasion. My solution is to be more organized. I put my stamps in accessible trays, keep my inks in my new rolling stack of drawers, file all piles of paper that otherwise turn my studio into an obstacle course, and keep my desk free of clutter.

Planning is my other organizational goal. January is always the longest month for me, so this time of year I use those long indoor hours to good advantage. In the beautiful Pacific Northwest, where I live, January is a seemingly endless succession of cold, gray, drizzly days. Planning for festive occasions in the year to come is a perfect way to lift my spirits during this dreary month.

Greeting Card Keepsake Book

MATERIALS

Chipboard, two 8-inch squares and two 7³⁄₄-inch squares

Decorative paper, two 10-inch squares, and two 9¹⁄₂-inch squares

Buff text-weight paper, two 8¹⁄₄-inch squares and six 16¹⁄₂-by-12¹⁄₄-inch pieces

Black card stock, 3⁷⁄₈ by 5¹⁄₈ inches

Buff card stock, 3⁵⁄₈ by 4⁷⁄₈ inches

Celadon, moss, and smoke blue pigment inks

Fred B. Mullett leaf stamp

This book will give you a tool for organizing a year's worth of birthday cards. It has twelve pockets for storing cards for each month and a space for recording the birth dates of friends and family. You can also adapt it for all special occasions.

1 Spray the wrong side of the two large pieces of decorative paper with spray adhesive. Cover the large pieces of chipboard with the paper for the front and back covers. Cut the corners at an angle and fold over each edge. Use a burnisher to smooth the paper. Repeat with the smaller pieces of decorative paper and chipboard to make the inside lining of the covers. Center and attach the linings to the unfinished side of each cover by spraying the smaller piece with spray adhesive.

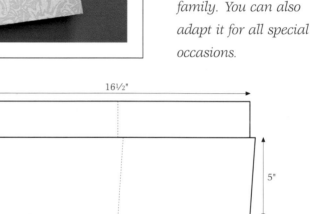

2 To make the inside pouch pages, measure five inches from the bottom of a large piece of the buff paper. Using a long straight edge and a scoring tool, score a fold line. Fold the lower edge up. Measure to find the center horizontally; score and fold, leaving the folded edges (the pouches) on the outside. Repeat these steps with the other five pieces.

3 Write the name of each month of the year on the top edge of each pouch. Use a straight edge and fine-tip pen to draw lines on the front of each pouch to record special dates.

4 To decorate the outside cover, stamp the leaf on the small buff paper. Glue the buff paper centered on the black paper and glue the black paper to the center of the cover.

5 Assemble the book by stacking the back cover, one 8¼-inch buff paper square, six folded pouch pages, the second 8¼-inch buff paper square, and the front cover. To bind the book, take it to your local printer (such as Kinko's) and ask for a spiral or wire binding. This relatively inexpensive binding will hold the book together, while allowing it to lie flat when open.

Leaf Thank You Note

Thank You Fold Note

Embossed Flower Card

Congratulations Card

JANUARY

Those long winter evenings in January are a perfect time to create a store of cards that you can send throughout the coming year. For someone who has sent a gift from far away, I like to offer my thanks with a special card that includes a photograph of me or a member of my family opening the package or wearing the gift. I also like to have some cards on hand that serve to acknowledge an accomplishment or a significant milestone in someone's life.

Leaf Thank You Note

MATERIALS

*Metallic silver card stock,
5 by 10 inches*

*Ivory card stock,
4 by 4 inches*

*Gold and silver
pigment inks*

Fred B. Mullett leaf stamp

Impress thank you *stamp*

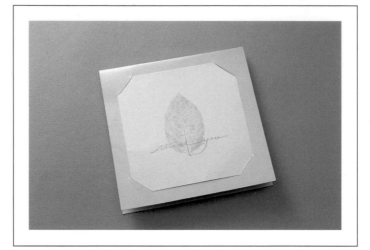

*With its simple leaf
motif, this note card is
appropriate for a special
occasion any time of the
year. It fits in a 5½-inch-
square envelope, which
costs slightly more to
mail, so check current
postage rates.*

1 Score a fold line on the silver card to make a folded five-inch-square card as shown in the illustration.

2 Using a pencil, lightly draw guidelines for four angled slits on the wrong side of the silver card. Cut the slits with an X-Acto knife. If you are making several cards, you may

want to make a template of the slits using a scrap of card stock. Lay the template over your silver card, secure both pieces with paper clips, and cut through the template slits.

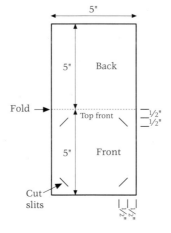

3 Stamp the leaf in silver on the ivory paper, and stamp *thank you* in gold.

4 Insert the stamped ivory paper through the slits. Fold and crease.

Embossed Flower Card

Layered papers add color and depth to this elegant pressure-embossed design.

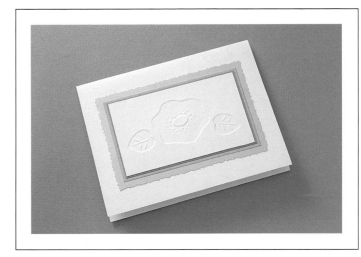

MATERIALS

*Ivory card stock,
5½ by 8½ inches and
2¼ by 3⅞ inches*

*Teal card stock,
2⅝ by 4⅛ inches*

*Light blue card stock,
2⅜ by 4 inches*

*Silver metallic card stock,
3¼ by 4¼ inches*

Silver pigment ink

Lasting Impressions flower embossing template

Impress thank you *stamp*

1 Score and fold the large ivory paper to form a folded card 4¼ by 5½ inches.

2 Pressure emboss the flower template in the center of the small ivory paper (see Pressure Embossing, page 6).

3 Center and glue the flower impression to the light blue paper, the light blue paper to the teal, and then the teal paper to the silver.

4 Trim the silver card with deckle-edge scissors to make a one-quarter-inch border around the teal paper.

5 Center and glue the colored layers to the front of the ivory card.

6 Finish the inside by stamping *thank you* in silver.

Thank You Fold Note

MATERIALS

*Ivory card stock,
5 by 11 inches*

*Silver pigment or clear
embossing ink*

Silver embossing powder

Turquoise pigment ink

*Rexel Derwent watercolor
pencils, kingfisher blue
(No. 38), May green
(No. 48), turquoise green
(No. 40)*

*Impress teacup square
and* thank you *stamps*

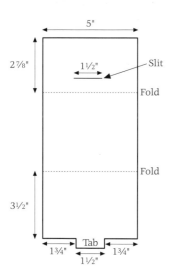

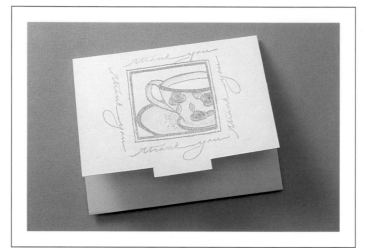

*Fold notes make great
additions to your
stationery supply. You
can make them in any
shape and size, and
because they are
self-mailers, they don't
require envelopes.*

1 Score and fold the ivory
paper as indicated in the
illustration.

2 Using an X-Acto knife,
cut a tab as shown in the
illustration.

3 Fold the card with the
tab end on the outside.
Make a pencil mark on
each side of the tab and cut
a slit using an X-Acto knife
and straight edge.

4 Stamp the teacup square
image in silver or clear
embossing ink, and apply
the silver embossing
powder.

5 Color the stamped image
with the watercolor pencils.

6 Stamp *thank you* in
turquoise along each side
of the square. Cover the
teacup square with a
straight piece of scrap

paper when you stamp
thank you on the top so the
tail of the *y* doesn't extend
over the image.

7 Fold and close by
inserting the tab through
the slit.

Congratulations Card

With these cheering hands you can applaud someone's special accomplishment, such as graduation or a new job. This card fits in a 5½-inch-square envelope.

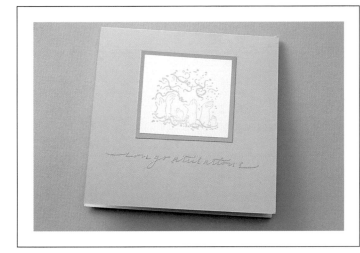

MATERIALS

Buff card stock, 5 by 10 inches

Metallic gold card stock, 2½ by 2½ inches

Ivory card stock, 2¼ by 2¼ inches

Silver pigment ink

Gold embossing ink

Gold embossing powder

Fine-tip metallic gold pen

Portfolio hands and confetti stamp

Impress congratulations stamp

1 Score a fold line on the buff paper to make a folded five-inch-square card.

2 Stamp hands and confetti on the ivory paper in silver. After the ink has dried, color the confetti with the metallic gold pen.

3 Glue the gold square to the front of the card, then glue the stamped ivory square in the center of the gold paper.

4 Stamp *congratulations* in embossing ink and sprinkle with gold embossing powder.

5 Fold and crease.

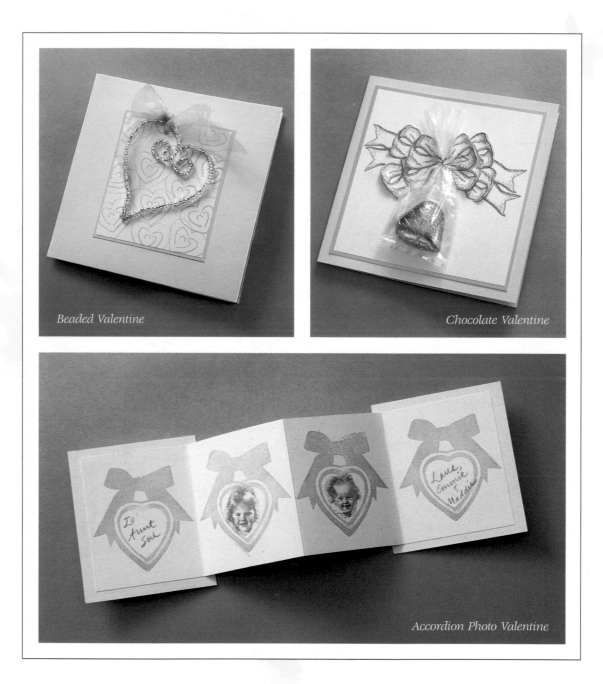

Beaded Valentine

Chocolate Valentine

Accordion Photo Valentine

18

FEBRUARY

A special sentiment, some sweets tied with a ribbon, a beautiful card. These are a few of my favorite ways to delight loved ones on the year's most sentimental holiday. If you haven't sent valentines to your friends for a few years, you might be surprised to find that adults enjoy them as much as children do. The bonus—you'll know you warmed the hearts of more than one "inner child."

Beaded Valentine

MATERIALS

*Light pink card stock,
5 by 10 inches*

*Ivory card stock,
2¾ by 3¼ inches*

*Metallic silver card stock,
2⅞ by 3⅜ inches*

*Gold and silver pigment
inks*

Impress heart spiral stamp

*Light pink, silver-lined glass
seed beads*

*Silver-colored 26-gauge wire,
15 inches long*

*Light pink, ¾-inch-wide
organdy ribbon, 12 inches
long*

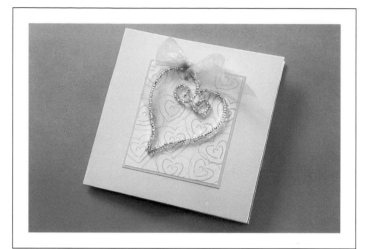

*Create a memento of a
day to remember with
this romantic beaded
and beribboned card.*

1 Score and fold the light
pink paper to make a five-
inch-square card.

2 Stamp the heart spiral
randomly in gold on the
ivory paper.

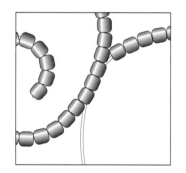

3 Crimp the end of the
wire and string about 11
inches of glass beads on the
wire. Following the illustration on the facing page,
shape the left side of the
heart. Then bend the wire
and work back up the right
side to where the two sides
come together at the top.

Feed the wire from the
right side through three of
the beads on the left wire
as shown. String another
1½ inches of beads on the
end of the wire and curl the
beaded wire on the right
side. Crimp the end of the
wire. Trim the excess wire
at both ends.

8 Finish the inside by stamping a valentine sentiment in silver.

4 Glue the small ivory paper to the center of the silver paper.

5 Punch a one-eighth-inch hole through the ivory and silver papers, 1¼ inches from the left edge and three-eighths of an inch from the top edge of the silver paper.

6 Feed the pink ribbon through the hole and through the left loop of the beaded heart. Tie a bow.

7 Center and glue the ivory and silver papers to the front of the folded pink card.

Chocolate Valentine

MATERIALS

*Light pink card stock,
5½ by 11 inches*

*Metallic silver card stock,
4⅞ by 4⅞ inches*

*Ivory card stock,
4⅝ by 4⅝ inches*

Rose and silver pigment inks

*Printworks bow and sweet
on you stamps*

Cellophane bag, 2 by 5 inches

Foil-covered chocolate heart

*Any chocolate lover
would be delighted with
the delicious treat
adorning this lovely
card. To mail it, use a
padded envelope.*

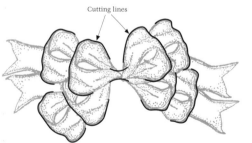

Cutting lines

1 Score and fold the light pink paper to make a 5½-inch-square card.

2 Begin stamping the loop of the bow in rose just right of center on the ivory paper using the masking technique (page 6). Make several masks for the ribbon loop. Continue stamping the loop, using the masks to create the bow as shown. Place masks over the outer loops and stamp the ribbon end twice on each side.

3 Using an X-ACTO knife, cut around the outer edge

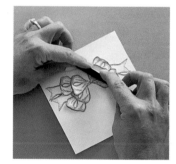

of each loop, and cut two slits across the center as shown in the illustration. Roll the cut edges of the ribbon loops around a pen to curl them forward.

4 Insert the chocolate heart into the cellophane bag; dab a bit of rubber cement behind the heart to hold it upright in the bag. Tightly pleat the top of the bag and slip it from the front through the lower slit

and back up through the top slit. Open and flare the top of the bag.

5 Center and glue the ivory paper to the silver paper, then glue both to the center of the pink card.

6 Finish the inside by stamping a valentine sentiment, such as Printworks' *sweet on you*, in silver.

Accordion Photo Valentine

When unfolded, this personalized valentine reveals photographs of two sweethearts of your choosing, framed in gold.

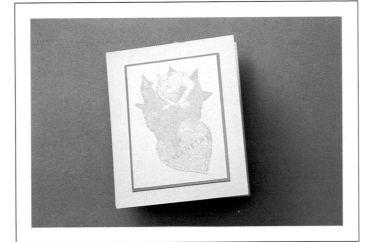

MATERIALS

Light pink card stock, two 2¼-by-2¾ inch pieces

Metallic gold paper, 2⁷⁄₁₆ by 3 inches

Ivory card stock, 2⅜ by 2⅞ inches and 11 by 3⅜ inches

Gold ink

Pink pen

Colorless blender pen

Impress rose pot valentine and ribbon heart frame stamps

Photocopies of two photographs

1 Stamp the rose pot valentine in gold on the small ivory paper.

2 Center and glue the stamped ivory paper to the gold paper. Center and glue the gold and ivory papers to the pink paper.

3 Score and fold the long ivory paper as shown in the illustration. Stamp the ribbon heart frames in gold, centered between each fold.

4 Write a sentiment in the first and last frames using a pink pen.

5 Use a colorless blender pen to transfer photocopies of your photos in the two middle frames (see Photo Transfer, page 6).

6 Glue the pink cards to each end of the accordion-fold paper.

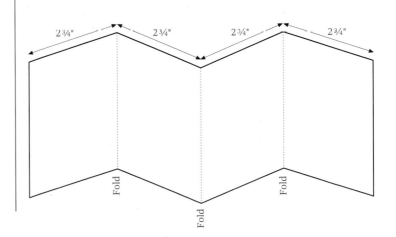

2¾" 2¾" 2¾" 2¾"

Fold Fold Fold

Balloon in a Slide Frame Card

Birthday Boy Card

Birthday Present Card

Fiftieth Birthday Card

Package Birthday Invitation

MARCH

Birthday cards—we probably send more of these than any

other card. This year, you can make birthdays for the

children and adults in your life a little more personal by

giving individually tailored, handmade cards. Such cards are

a gift in themselves, the sort of treasure that may well end

up in a family scrapbook.

Balloon in a Slide Frame Card

MATERIALS

White card stock,
5½ by 11 inches

Heavyweight vellum,
1½ by 1¾ inches

Black pigment ink

Clear embossing powder

Turquoise marker

Hero Arts balloon stamp

Black slide frame

Turquoise, 1½-inch-wide
organdy ribbon,
12 inches long

Slide-transparency holders make perfect frames for tiny stamped images on cards. You can also use them to make magnets or gift tags.

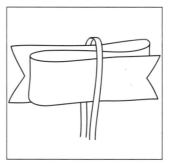

1 Score and fold the white paper in half to form a 5½-inch-square card.

2 With the fold of the card at the top, stamp balloons in black.

3 Stamp a balloon in the center of the vellum in black and heat emboss with clear embossing powder.

4 Color the balloon on vellum with the turquoise marker. Slip the vellum into the slide frame.

5 To make a bow, cut a four-inch length of ribbon. Cut the ribbon lengthwise to a width of about one-quarter inch. Form a bow with the longer uncut ribbon and tie it with the narrow piece as shown in the illustration. Tape the narrow ribbon tie to the

white card; it will be covered by the slide frame.

6 Using double-stick mounting tape, attach the slide to the center of the card.

7 Stamp a birthday sentiment in black inside the card.

Birthday Boy Card

This whimsical cake lover will delight birthday boys and girls of any age.

MATERIALS

Ivory card stock, 5½ by 8½ inches and 2 by 2⅜ inches

Black card stock, 3 by 2¾ inches

Black and gold pigment inks

Clear embossing powder

Cream, blush pink, light orange, and turquoise colored pencils

All Night Media cake boy stamp

Hero Arts swirl stamp

1 Score and fold the large ivory paper.

2 Stamp the cake boy in black in the center of the small ivory paper and heat emboss with clear embossing powder. Color the face, cake, and plate with colored pencils.

3 Using a foam cosmetics sponge or dauber, smudge the gold pigment ink on the background to the edge of the paper, leaving the area around the figure clear.

4 Trim the black card with deckle-edge scissors.

5 Center and glue the stamped card to the black card.

6 Randomly stamp the swirl in gold on the front of the ivory card.

7 Center and glue the stamped cards to the center of the ivory card.

8 Stamp a birthday sentiment inside in black.

Fiftieth Birthday Card

MATERIALS

*Black card stock,
6½ by 11 inches*

*Ivory card stock,
8½ by 11 inches*

*Metallic silver card stock,
2½ by 5½ inches*

Black pigment ink

White shipping tag

*Hot Potatoes number
stamps*

*Impress Happy Birthday
stamp*

*This striking card is
an emphatic way to
recognize the passage of
The Big Five-O or any
other of those significant
decades.*

1 Stamp the appropriate
year (50 in this case) in
black on the white tag.

2 Score and fold the black
paper in half, to 5½ by
6½ inches.

3 Type about 15 lines of
*fifty the big five-o one-half
century* on a computer; it
looks best if the words are
not lined up. For the font, I
used 24-point Cezanne
(made by Type Foundry).
Print the text on the ivory
paper. Trim to 4¼ by 5½
inches.

4 Center and glue the
printed ivory paper to the
front of the black card.

5 Tape the end of the tag
strings to the back side of

the silver paper, and glue
the silver to the center of
the printed ivory paper.

6 Stamp *Happy Birthday*
inside in silver.

28

Birthday Present Card

A birthday card should be just as special as the occasion. This card is designed to actually look like a gift. The bow stamp is the same one used on the chocolate valentine card.

MATERIALS

Ivory card stock, 6 by 8 inches

Yellow, corded shipping tag, 1⅜ by 2¾ inches

Yellow and aqua dye inks

Aqua colored pencil

Printworks ribbon stamp

Magenta polka dot stamp

Rubber Stampede alphabet stamps

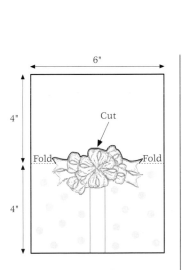

1 On the ivory paper, measure the halfway point along each edge and mark with a pencil.

2 Stamp the ribbon in aqua so that the top of the ribbon is about one-half inch above the halfway point. You may want to use the masking technique (page 6).

3 Using a straight edge and the aqua pencil, extend the ribbon down the center of the package. Color all the ribbons with the aqua pencil.

4 Stamp polka dots in yellow.

5 Using an X-ACTO knife, cut along the top of the ribbon that extends above the halfway point of the card as shown in the illustration.

6 Score from the end of the ribbon to each side of the card and fold.

7 Stamp or write the recipient's name in aqua on the yellow tag. Trim the string, tape the ends to the back of the tag, and glue the tag on the ivory card as shown.

8 Stamp *Happy Birthday* in aqua inside.

Package Birthday Invitation

MATERIALS

*Turquoise card stock,
5½ by 11 inches*

*Ivory card stock,
4 by 4 inches and
4¼ by 5 inches*

*Yellow card stock,
4¼ by 4¼ inches*

Aqua and black dye inks

*Light aqua and yellow
colored pencils*

*Stamps by Judith large
package stamp*

*DeNami party invitation
stamp*

*This package card has a
pocket inside that you
can use in many ways.
You can substitute a
birthday wish and a
monetary gift for the
invitation, or make the
card in Christmas colors
and insert a photograph.*

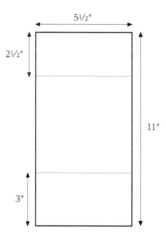

1 Score and fold the
turquoise paper as shown.

2 Stamp the package in
aqua in the center of the

four-inch square of ivory
paper. Color the stripes on
the package with a yellow
pencil.

3 Center the ivory paper
square over the yellow one
and glue.

4 Center the ivory and
yellow papers on the front
of the folded turquoise
card. On the yellow paper,
mark with a pencil the
point where the ends of the
turquoise card meet.

5 Using a paper cutter, cut
through both the yellow
and ivory papers at the
pencil mark.

6 Glue the cut papers on
the front of the turquoise
card.

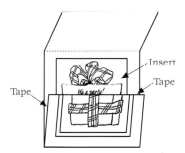

9 Stamp the party invitation in black inside the box. Insert this card into the pocket.

7 Open the card and apply a piece of double-stick tape on each outside edge on the bottom half of the card and press together. This creates the pocket for the invitation.

8 Carefully clean the package stamp. Using the aqua dye pad, ink only the box-top segment of the package. Stamp the box top at the top of the remaining piece of ivory paper. Finish the outline of the box with a light aqua pencil.

Ribbon Rose Card

Carrots in a Pot Card

Checkered Flowers Thank You Card

Birdhouse Gift Tag

Handmade Gift Bag

April

This is it—spring! We've made it through the long winter months and our gardens are beginning to sprout an array of colors. We can officially dress in pastels, plan festive celebrations, and brighten someone's life with cards in Easter egg colors. Your beautiful creations will be a match for the month's tulips, daffodils, and other blooms.

Ribbon Rose Card

MATERIALS

Turquoise card stock,
5½ by 8½ inches

Ivory card stock,
2⅝ by 3¼ inches

Metallic gold card stock,
2¾ by 3½ inches

Moss pigment ink

Clear embossing powder

Metallic gold pen

Turquoise wired-ribbon rose

Impress wavy square
frame stamp

A nostalgic ribbon rose
in a modern setting
creates a fresh look for
this spring note card.

1 Score and fold the turquoise paper to make a folded card, 5½ by 4¼ inches.

2 Stamp the wavy square frame in moss, approximately one-half inch from the top.

3 Heat emboss with clear embossing powder.

4 Attach the ribbon rose to the card by making one stitch from back to front with a needle and thread. Secure the thread ends in back with adhesive tape.

5 Draw random dots with the gold pen around the ribbon rose inside the green wavy square.

6 Write or stamp *happy spring* in gold beneath the wavy square.

7 Center and glue the ivory paper to the gold, then glue both on front of the turquoise card, three-quarters of an inch from the top, centered horizontally.

Checkered Flowers Thank You Card

Shades of olive and turquoise give this card a spring look, but the design is suitable for any time of year.

MATERIALS

Light olive-green card stock, 5½ by 8½ inches

Turquoise card stock, 2 by 4⅛ inches

Ivory card stock, 1⅞ by 4 inches

Moss, turquoise, and white pigment inks

Imaginations sponged square and bouquet stamps

Impress thank you stamp

1 Fold and score the green paper to 4¼ by 5½ inches.

2 Stamp the sponged square stamp along the ivory paper in moss.

3 Stamp the tiny bouquet in turquoise in the spaces between the squares.

4 Center and glue the ivory paper onto the turquoise, then glue these pieces on the front of the green card, 1½ inches from the lower edge, centered horizontally.

5 Stamp *thank you* in white, centered below the turquoise.

Carrots in a Pot Card

MATERIALS

Light olive-green card stock,
4¼ by 11 inches

Turquoise card stock,
3½ by 4½ inches

White card stock,
approximately 3 by 6 inches

Purple and gold
pigment inks

Fawn dye ink

Purple colored pencil

Orange and light green
brush markers

Gold metallic pen

Co-Motion flower pot stamp

Posh Impressions
carrot stamp

Rubber Stamps of America
bunny stamp

Renaissance Rubber Happy
Easter stamp

When you open this
card, you'll pull up the
carrots to find a bunny
hiding inside.

1 Score and fold the olive-green paper as shown in the illustration.

2 Using an X-Acto knife, notch the card as shown.

3 On the white paper, stamp the flower pot in purple, and color it with a purple pencil. Cut around the pot, close to the line.

4 Ink the carrot stamp with the orange and light green brush markers. Stamp three times on the remaining white paper, approximately one-quarter inch apart, re-inking each time. Cut around the carrots, leaving them attached where the greens overlap.

5 Cut wavy edges along the turquoise paper as shown. The finished size should be approximately 3 by 4¼ inches.

6 Fold the bottom (larger part) of the green card up, and fold the top down; they will overlap. Center the turquoise paper over the green paper and mark a line with a pencil where the lower edge of the top runs beneath the turquoise paper. Cut along the line.

Mark and cut.

Gold dots

With the green paper folded closed, glue the turquoise pieces to the top and bottom of the green paper.

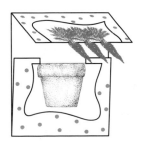

7 Draw random gold dots on the front of the green paper.

8 Glue the flower pot to the lower half of the turquoise paper, aligned with the bottom of the notch. Glue the carrots to the top half of the turquoise paper.

9 Stamp the bunny inside the card with fawn dye ink. The bunny's head should appear to be looking out of

the pot when the top part of the card is open. Stamp *Happy Easter* beneath the bunny in gold.

10 To close the card, slip the carrots into the notch.

Handmade Gift Bag

MATERIALS

*Pale green gift wrap
or butcher paper,
14 by 14 inches*

Teal pigment ink

Fred B. Mullett salal stamp

*Turquoise, 1½-inch-wide
organdy ribbon,
about 36 inches long*

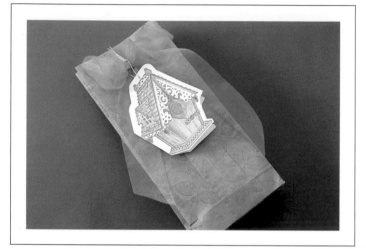

*With a rubber stamp
and gift wrap or butcher
paper, you can create a
beautiful handmade bag
for any gift. Practice with
butcher paper first,
experimenting with
different sizes and
proportions.*

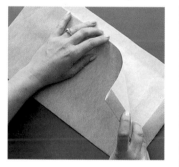

1 With right side facing
down, fold the top edge of
the paper down one inch
and glue. (The instructions
in steps 1–11 follow the
numbered illustrations.)

2 Fold right side to left.
The left side should extend
one inch beyond the right.
Crease and fold.

3 Fold a one-inch extension (left side) over the
right side and crease.

4 Slip the right side
beneath the folded exten-
sion and glue.

5 Measure one inch from
either side and score a fold
line. Fold and crease.

6 Reverse folds and crease.
This forms the gusset of
the bag.

7 Fold and crease four
inches from lower edge.

8 Lift the lower fold. Use
both index fingers to form
and crease a triangular fold
at each gusset.

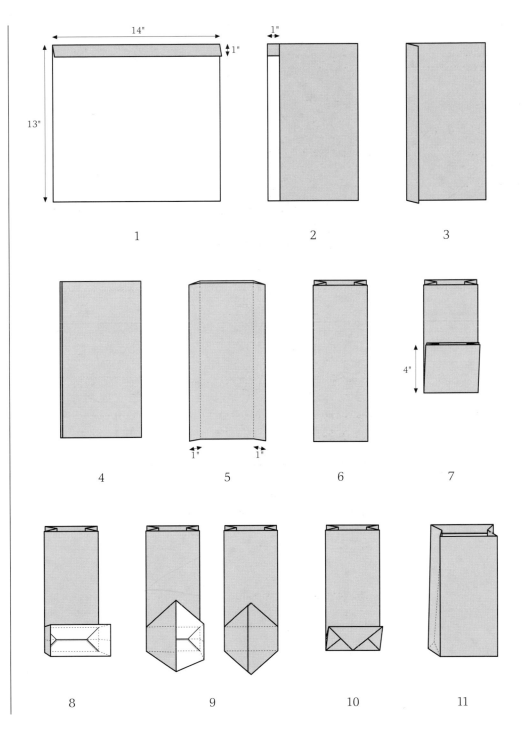

9 Fold the left side flat; repeat with the right side.

10 Fold the upper and lower flaps down and glue.

11 With the bag lying flat, stamp the salal leaf randomly in teal.

12 Wrap the turquoise ribbon around the bag lengthwise and tie a ribbon. Tie the birdhouse gift tag (pages 40–41) to the ribbon with silver cord.

Birdhouse Gift Tag

MATERIALS

*Ivory card stock,
8½ by 11 inches*

Turquoise pigment ink

Brown dye ink

*Clear embossing powder,
ultra-thick*

*Chartreuse, olive, and
purple watercolor pencils
and watercolor brush*

*Tan, chartreuse, and
turquoise colored pencils*

*Personal Stamp Exchange
Victorian birdhouse stamp*

*Uptown special delivery
bird stamp*

Silver cord, 6 inches long

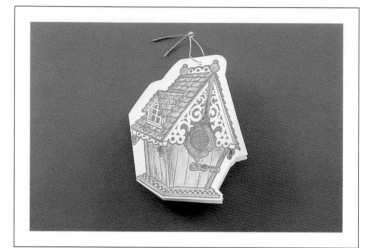

*When you tie this gift
tag to the front of the
leaf-covered bag with a
big bow, it evokes a
birdhouse perched in a
leafy tree. Open the tag
and a little bird pops out
with a letter that says
"for you."*

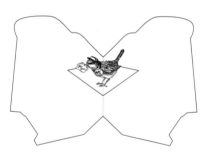

1 On the ivory paper,
stamp the birdhouse in
turquoise and heat emboss
with embossing powder. Be
sure to leave enough space
around the stamped image
to fold the card.

2 Score a fold line
parallel to the left
edge of the lower
half of the bird-
house. Fold and
crease. Use scissors
to cut a one-quarter-
inch border around
the birdhouse,
cutting through
both layers of the card.

3 Use chartreuse, olive,
and purple watercolor
pencils to paint the
birdhouse. The watercolor
brush allows you to push
the color right up against
the thick lines created by
the ultra-thick embossing
powder.

4 On the remaining ivory
paper, stamp the special
delivery bird in brown.
Color with tan, chartreuse,
and turquoise colored
pencils. Trim the paper
close to the design.

5 On the remaining paper,
cut a wedge as shown in
the illustration. Score and
fold the wedge on the
dashed lines.

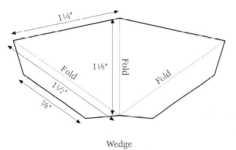

Wedge

6 Fold back the lower tabs of the wedge. Apply rubber cement to the tabs only and position as shown. Line up the fold lines of the wedge inside the gift tag. As you close the gift tag, the wedge shape should fold toward you.

7 Glue the bird to the right side of the wedge. Before the rubber cement dries, be sure that the bird doesn't show when the card is closed. If it does, reposition it on the wedge.

8 Punch a hole through both layers at the top of the gift tag. Using a piece of silver cord, tie the gift tag to the bow on the gift bag.

Alphabet Bead Baby Card

Woven Ribbon Card

Baby Shower Invitation

Baby Shower Favor Package

MAY

Oh baby! Whether you're congratulating someone else or announcing your own little bundle of love, you'll want a unique card to express your joy. And don't forget Mother's Day. The woven ribbon card is a beautiful way to honor Mom on her special day.

Alphabet Bead Baby Card

MATERIALS

*Pale blue card stock,
5 by 7 inches and
1½ by 2 inches*

*Lightweight vellum,
2¼ by 4 inches*

White pigment ink

Black dye ink

*Darcie's Country Folk
solid stripe stamp*

Silver eyelets, 4

*Birth announcement or
congratulations stamps*

Alphabet beads

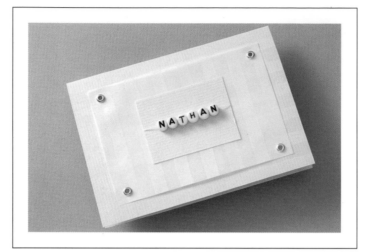

*This card, with the
baby's name spelled in
tiny beads, is sure to
become a treasured
keepsake.*

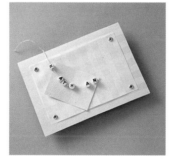

1 Score and fold the large blue paper to 3½ by 5 inches.

2 On the front of the blue paper, stamp the horizontal solid stripes in white, about one-quarter inch apart, beginning one-quarter inch from the top.

3 Repeat the white stripes vertically on the vellum.

4 Center the vellum over the blue paper. The vertical over horizontal white stripes should create a plaid pattern through the vellum. Punch one-eighth-inch holes in each corner of the vellum through the blue card. Affix an eyelet in each hole to hold the vellum and blue paper together (see Creative Fasteners, page 8).

5 Using a needle and thread, string alphabet beads that spell the baby's name. Center the beads over the small blue paper, and tape the string ends to the back.

6 Center and glue the beaded card to the vellum.

7 For an announcement, use a birth information stamp inside and fill in the blanks. For a baby card, stamp *congratulations* inside in black.

Baby Shower Invitation

I love the contrast between the industrial shipping tag and the soft colors and ribbon on this baby shower invitation. Its simplicity makes it beautiful, yet easy to mass produce. Use a vellum business-size envelope for mailing.

MATERIALS

Light pink card stock, 4 1/8 by 8 1/4 inches

Cream-colored, 4-by-8-inch shipping tag

Fawn dye ink

Pink colored pencil

Mostly Animals baby boots stamp

Impress invitation stamp

Pink, 3/4-inch-wide organdy ribbon, 10 inches long

1 Using a paper cutter, trim one-eighth inch off each long side of the tag.

2 Stamp baby boots in fawn on the tag.

3 Lightly color the baby boots with the pink pencil.

4 Stamp the invitation stamp in fawn approximately one inch from the bottom of the tag.

5 Use the pink pencil to write *Baby Shower* above the invitation stamp.

6 Lay the tag over the pink card, with the top edges aligned. Punch a hole through the tag hole and the pink card.

7 Feed the pink ribbon through the holes and tie a double knot. Trim the ribbon ends at an angle.

Woven Ribbon Card

MATERIALS

*Ivory card stock,
11 by 5½ inches and
3¼ by 3¾ inches*

*Pink card stock,
3½ by 4 inches*

Gold pigment ink

*Platinum pink pearlescent
liquid acrylic or pink
colored pencil*

Olive-green colored pencil

*Imaginations swirl rose
stamp*

*Gold, ¾-inch-wide organdy
ribbon, 12 inches long*

*This delicate floral and
organdy design is
suitable for Mother's
Day, a baby card, or a
wedding.*

1 Score and fold the large ivory paper to make a 5½-inch-square card.

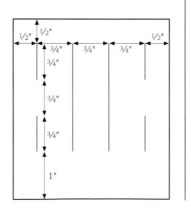

2 Using a pencil and ruler, transfer the markings in the illustration to the back of the smaller ivory paper. Cut slits as indicated with an X-ACTO knife and straight edge.

3 Turn the card over and weave the ribbon through as shown. Attach the ribbon to the back with rubber cement.

Ribbon

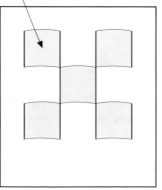

4 Stamp the swirl rose in gold in each of the four spaces.

5 Use the pink pearlescent liquid acrylic (or pink pencil) to color the stamped roses. Color the leaves with the olive-green pencil.

6 Center and glue the small ivory paper to the pink paper and the pink paper to the front of the folded ivory card.

7 Stamp a Mother's Day or other event greeting inside in gold.

46

Baby Shower Favor Package

Tied with a little plastic pacifier charm and filled with a treat or gift, this traditional Japanese folded package makes a great party favor for baby shower guests. Vary the colors and stamp to customize the design for any occasion.

MATERIALS

White text-weight paper or gift wrap, 8½ by 10½ inches

Pale aqua dye ink

Mostly Animals baby feet stamp

Baby blue, 1½-inch-wide organdy ribbon, 25 inches long

Plastic pacifier charm

1 On the paper, measure and cut the tab as shown in the illustration.

2 Score fold lines.

3 Randomly stamp baby feet in pale aqua.

4 Turn the paper over so the stamped side is away from you. Fold the paper toward you along the horizontal scored fold lines.

5 Open the paper flat and fold toward you along the vertical scored fold lines. Repeat along all the diagonal fold lines, this time folding away from you (opposite of the horizontal fold).

6 With the tab at the top, fold both vertical folds toward you. Now bring the top (tab end) and bottom together, collapsing along the diagonal fold lines.

7 Bring the tab over the top, wrap a ribbon around the package, and tie. Slip the pacifier charm onto the ribbon and tie a bow.

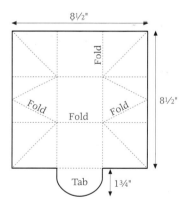

8½"

Fold

Fold

Fold

Fold

Fold

8½"

Tab

1¾"

Romantic Wedding Card

Bridal Shower Invitation

Angel Wedding Card

Wedding Invitation & Reception Card

Father's Day Card

48

JUNE

In June our thoughts turn to love, commitment, and grand events. Whether you are planning a wedding or celebrating the anniversary of a couple who have become a memorable duo, you'll want to acknowledge the occasion with a romantic card. A soft, elegant approach is just right.

Romantic Wedding Card

MATERIALS

*Ivory card stock,
6 by 9½ inches*

*Lightweight vellum,
8½ by 11 inches*

Gold pigment ink

Gold heart sticker

*Ivory, 1½-inch-wide
double-faced satin ribbon,
18 inches long*

Silver heart charm

*This lush design will
embellish any wedding
or anniversary gift. It
also makes a beautiful
valentine.*

1 Score and fold the ivory paper to 6 by 4¾ inches.

2 Fold the vellum in half and trace the heart shape.

3 Cut out the heart using scallop-edge scissors. Cut through both layers of the vellum, but not along the fold.

4 Place the vellum heart over the ivory card so that one side lies on the front of the card and one on the back.

5 Affix the gold sticker on the vellum heart.

6 Using a needle and thread, sew the heart charm through the vellum and sticker. Secure the thread on the back of the vellum with adhesive tape.

7 Tie the satin ribbon into a bow and attach it to the top of the card with double-stick mounting foam.

8 Stamp a wedding (or valentine) sentiment inside in gold.

9 Trim one-quarter inch off the bottom front of the card with a paper cutter.

10 To make the gold border, open the card and lay a piece of scrap paper along the bottom inside edge. The mask should be parallel to the lower edge of the card, three-eighths of an inch from the bottom. Using a foam sponge, smudge gold ink along the masked edge of the card. Be sure to put scrap paper beneath the card to protect your work surface.

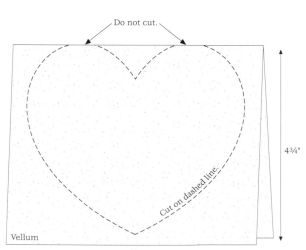

Do not cut.

Cut on dashed line.

4¾"

Vellum

Bridal Shower Invitation

Choosing a theme for a bridal shower makes it easier for your guests to select a gift and allows you to coordinate the invitations and decor. To change the theme, just use different stamps.

MATERIALS

Ivory card stock, 3¼ by 3⅝ inches and 4¼ by 5 inches

Yellow card stock, 4¼ by 4½ inches and 4¼ by 5½ inches

Olive-green dye ink

Fine-tip black pen

Stamp Francisco watering can stamp

Impress bridal shower *and* invitation *stamps*

Graven Images flower pot stamp

Rubber Stamps of America shovel stamp

Yellow, ¾-inch-wide organdy ribbon, 12 inches long

1 Stamp the watering can in olive-green just below center on the small ivory paper.

2 Stamp *bridal shower* in olive-green along the lower edge of the large ivory card and the invitation information centered vertically and to the left (to allow space for writing).

3 On the large yellow paper, stamp the flower pot approximately three-quarters of an inch from the lower edge.

4 With a fine-tip black pen write *Let's fill _____ 's garden!* Just above the writing, stamp the shovel in olive-green.

5 Layer the papers, beginning with the largest piece on the bottom. The top edges of the three largest cards should be aligned. Center the smallest ivory paper over the smallest yellow paper.

6 Hold all four pieces together and punch two holes through all layers at the top edge, centered. Feed the organdy ribbon through the holes and tie a bow in front.

Angel Wedding Card

MATERIALS

Pre-made ivory card, folded size 6¾ by 4½ inches

Gold pigment ink

Gold embossing powder

Marks of Distinction angel stamp

Hero Arts heart stamp

White, 3-inch-wide organdy ribbon, 8 inches long

An angel with heart in hand, floating on sheer organdy. This card celebrates love with dreamy charm.

1 Stamp the angel in gold in the center of the ribbon. Set aside to dry.

2 Place the angel design over the card and position the heart to appear to be in her hand. Stamp the heart on the card in gold. Heat emboss with gold embossing powder.

3 Lightly stamp several more hearts in gold on the card so the angel appears to be flying through them.

4 Attach the ribbon to the center of the card (positioned so that the embossed heart is in the angel's hand) by smearing a dab of glue from a glue stick at either end of the card. Gently press the ribbon over the glued area.

5 Trim the ribbon ends close to the card edges.

Father's Day Card

An important day like Father's Day is not to be forgotten, even amid the excitement of weddings. My dad always referred to himself as "the king," so this card is a perfect tribute to him on his special day.

MATERIALS

Pale-green ribbed card stock, 8 by 8½ inches

Black card stock, 2¼ by 3⅛ inches

Ivory card stock, 2 by 2⅞ inches

Gold pigment ink

Gold embossing powder

Black dye ink

Black pen

Personal Stamp Exchange large crown stamp

Stamp Francisco large diamond stamp

Impress Happy Father's Day stamp

1 Score and fold the green paper to make a card that is 4 by 8½ inches.

2 Stamp the large crown in gold in the center of the ivory paper. Heat emboss with gold embossing powder.

3 Use double-stick mounting foam to adhere the ivory paper to the center of the black paper.

4 On the front of the green card, stamp large diamonds in gold, beginning in the upper left corner.

5 Glue the ivory and black papers to the front of the green card, approximately 2¼ inches from the top, centered horizontally.

6 On the inside, stamp *Happy Father's Day* in black, then write *to the king* with the black pen.

Wedding Invitation & Reception Card

MATERIALS

*Pale yellow card stock,
6¾ by 8½ inches*

*Lightweight vellum,
8½ by 11 inches*

White pigment ink

White embossing powder

*Darcie's Country Folk solid
stripe stamp*

*White, 1½-inch-wide
organdy ribbon, 12 inches
long*

Small silver heart charm

*Designing your own
wedding invitation will
ensure that you get exactly
the look you want. Before
you decide the card size,
make sure you can get
matching envelopes. The
information sheet can be
printed on your computer
printer or by a
professional printer.*

Punched holes

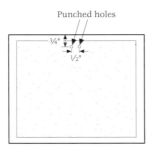

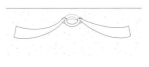

WEDDING INVITATION

1 Use a computer and a
fancy font (this one is a
formal script) to compose

the invitation information.
Print on 8½-by-11-inch
vellum and trim to 6 by 7½
inches.

2 Stamp the solid stripes
vertically, one-quarter inch
apart, in white on yellow
paper. Heat emboss with
white embossing powder.

3 Center the vellum over
the yellow paper. Punch
two one-quarter-inch holes,
one-half inch apart and
three-quarters of an inch
from the top, centered,
through both layers.

4 Thread the ribbon
through the holes from the
front to back, then back to
front as shown in the
illustration.

5 Sew the silver heart
charm to the center of the
ribbon with needle and
thread. Tie off and tuck the
knot behind the ribbon.

MATERIALS

*Pale yellow card stock,
5½ by 4⅛ inches*

*Lightweight vellum,
8½ by 11 inches*

White pigment ink

White embossing powder

*Inkadinkadoo large swirl
stamp*

Heart buttons, 2

RECEPTION CARD

1 Stamp the swirl in white
on yellow paper and heat
emboss with white
embossing powder.

2 Print the wedding reception information on
8½-by-11-inch vellum and
trim to 4⅞ by 3½ inches.

3 Dab glue on the upper
corners of the vellum and
glue it to the yellow paper.

4 Affix heart buttons to the
top corners of the vellum
with double-stick mounting
foam.

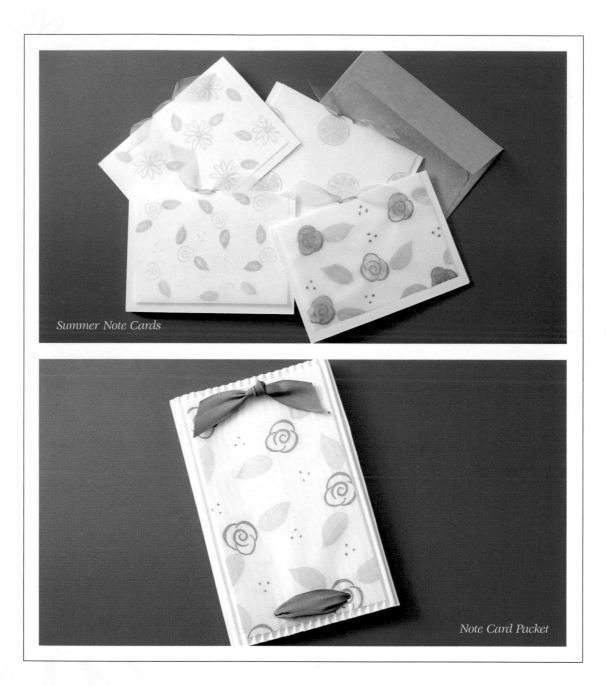

Summer Note Cards

Note Card Packet

JULY

The July of my dreams is a string

of long, warm, carefree days. The colorful

note cards that follow reflect the playful mood of summer.

Wrapped in the coordinating packet, they make a great

handmade gift that will brighten anyone's mood all

year long.

Summer Note Cards

MATERIALS

Makes one each of the four designs.

Ivory card stock,
four 6¼-by-9-inch pieces

Lightweight vellum,
four 5¾-by-8½-inch pieces

Pink, pale aqua, olive-green,
black, purple, and yellow
dye inks

Lavender and purple
watercolor pencils

Impress stamps: daisy,
small swirl rose, three-dot,
small leaf, large swirl rose,
large leaf, citrus half-slice,
and citrus full-slice

Olive-green, ¾-inch-wide
organdy ribbon,
36 inches long

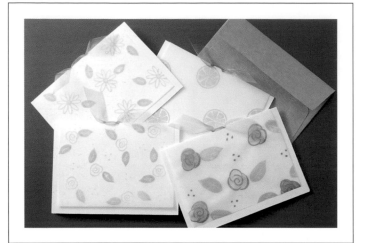

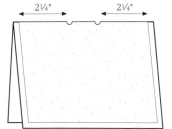

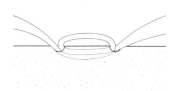

2¼"   2¼"

*A set of these cards
makes a thoughtful gift.
They can be stamped
with* thank you, happy
birthday, *or* congratulations, *or left blank and
packaged with flower
postage stamps.*

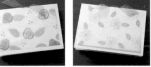

1 Score and fold the ivory paper to 4½ by 6¼ inches. Fold the vellum to 4¼ by 5¾ inches.

2 For the daisy and small rose cards, randomly stamp daisies in pink and small roses in pale aqua, and stamp the small solid leaf in olive-green on the inside of the vellum. For the rose card, stamp the three-dot stamp in pale aqua between the flowers. Allow 20 to 30 minutes for the ink to

dry thoroughly on all the vellum pieces. You can speed the drying time by blowing on the ink with a heat gun.

3 For the large rose card, stamp the rose in black on the inside of the vellum, and stamp the large solid leaf in olive-green. Color the large roses with lavender and purple watercolor pencils on the inside of the vellum. Fill in with the three-dot stamp in purple.

4 For the lemon-lime card, stamp the citrus half-slice in yellow and the full-slice in olive on the inside of the vellum.

5 Lay the vellum over the ivory card, centered, so there is a one-quarter-inch margin on both sides and at the lower (open) edge.

6 Using a one-quarter-inch-hole punch, make two holes along the folded edge of the card, punching through both vellum and card stock, as shown in the illustration.

7 Thread nine-inch-long pieces of the organdy ribbon through the holes, from front to back and back to front (see illustration).

Note Card Packet

This very simple folder makes an elegant package for your stationery gift.

MATERIALS

White, wide corrugated paper, 8 by 13 inches

Lightweight vellum, 4½ by 7½ inches

Black pigment ink

Olive-green and purple dye inks

Impress large swirl rose, solid leaf, and three-dot stamps

Olive-green, ⅞-inch-wide grosgrain ribbon, 18 inches long

1 Stamp the rose randomly in black on the vellum. To make this random stamping appear natural, turn the stamp slightly each time it is stamped. Allow to dry thoroughly, then stamp the leaf in olive-green. Stamp the three-dots between the roses in purple.

2 Corrugated paper usually comes rolled, so you may want to roll it in the opposite direction to make it lie flat. With the corrugated side down, place the stack of four note cards and envelopes on the paper, approximately three inches from the right edge. Wrap the right side over the note cards and bring the left side over the top.

3 Following the illustration, mark holes on the front with a pencil. Punch the holes through the front. Insert a pencil through these holes to mark hole location for the side flap and back. The right-side holes will be lined up for front, side flap, and back.

4 Lay the vellum, stamped side down, centered over the front of the corrugated paper. Punch four holes in line with the holes on the packet. Thread the ribbon through the holes in the packet and the vellum, beginning at the bottom front, then through the top from back to front. Tie a bow in front.

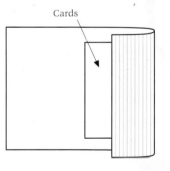

Cards

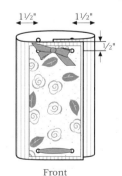

1½"   1½"   ½"

Front

Back

Bee Card

Bee Book Cover

RE AD

Bee Pillow

Pivoting Sunshine Card

YOU

Paper Coasters and Take-Out Boxes

AUGUST

Languid, sunshiny afternoons tempt us to while away the hours reading a good book in this last full month of summer. Bees seem to symbolize days like these, buzzing about our gardens and occasionally cruising through our picnics. This month's projects highlight these images of summer.

Bee Card

MATERIALS

*Black card stock,
3³⁄₄ by 3¹⁄₄ inches*

*Pale yellow card stock,
4¹⁄₄ by 9¹⁄₄ inches*

*· Heavy text-weight ivory
paper, 17 by 4 inches*

Heavyweight vellum

Black pigment ink

Clear embossing powder

*Black, small-nib, felt-tip
calligraphy pen*

Yellow colored pencil

TooMuchFun bee stamp

*Hot Potatoes alphabet
stamps*

*Personal Stamp Exchange
flying bee stamp*

Eyelets, 2

*Use this card to offer a
word of encouragement
to someone special in
your life.*

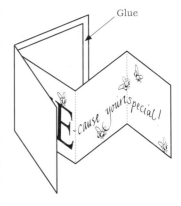

1 Stamp the large
bee in black on
heavy vellum, and
emboss with clear
embossing powder.
Trim to approxi-
mately 3¹⁄₂ inches
horizontally and
3 inches vertically,
centering the bee
image.

2 Score and fold the yellow
paper in half.

3 Center the black paper
on the yellow, center the

bee-stamped vellum over
the black paper, and attach
both with eyelets.

4 For the inside of the
card, measure 4¹⁄₄ inches
from the left side of the
ivory paper and score a fold
line.

5 Using black pigment ink
and alphabet stamps, stamp
BEE, beginning just to the
right of the score mark.
Let the ink dry before
proceeding. Using the callig-

raphy pen, write—*cause
you're special!* after *BEE*.

6 Stamp the little flying
bee in black, from the word
BEE to the right border of
the paper, several times in
a zigzag pattern. Allow to
dry, then color with a
yellow pencil.

7 Make two more score
lines at 4¹⁄₄-inch intervals.
Glue and fold as shown.

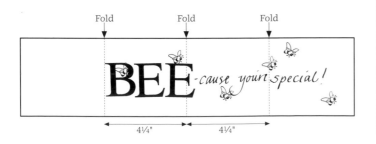

Bee Book Cover

Reading a paperback book at the pool or beach is a special rite of summer. Whether you want to protect your paperback or to hide your taste in pulp fiction, this stamped fabric cover will do the job with style.

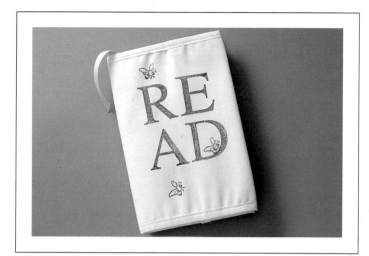

MATERIALS

Cotton prefinished book cover

Black permanent fabric ink

Yellow permanent fabric marker

Hot Potatoes alphabet stamps

Personal Stamp Exchange bee stamp

1 On the book cover, stamp *READ* in black using the alphabet stamps. Stamp the bee above the R, inside the D, and below the A.

2 Color the bee with a yellow permanent fabric marker.

3 When the ink is dry, iron the image on the wrong side to set the ink.

Pivoting Sunshine Card

MATERIALS

Yellow-gold card stock, 8½ by 11 inches

Black dye ink

Gold pigment ink

Leavenworth Jackson circle face stamp

Rubber Stampede alphabet stamps

Marks of Distinction Olivia sun stamp

The image on the front of this cleverly folded card moves as you open the card so the gaze of the enigmatic face follows you as the card opens to the inside.

1 Score and fold the yellow paper vertically to make a folded card, 5½ by 8½ inches. Score and fold horizontally to 4¼ by 5½ inches.

2 Unfold the card and measure the folding and stamping lines as shown in the illustration. Mark lightly with a pencil.

3 Using a straight edge and X-Acto knife, cut both horizontal slits.

4 Stamp the circle face in black, centering it over the 2⅛-inch mark and between the horizontal slits.

5 Score from the left end of the upper slit to the top of the face design; repeat for the bottom slit. Score a vertical line between the right end of the slits.

6 Cut along the left half of the circle face with an X-Acto knife.

7 Fold the card in half and cut along the previous semicircular cut, this time cutting through both layers.

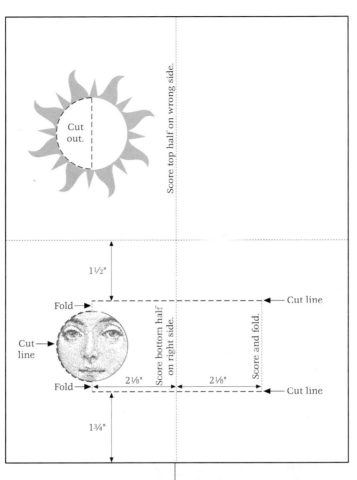

8 Fold the card closed, folding the flap between the slashes toward you, and inserting the circle face through the hole.

9 Transfer the sun-rays design in the illustration onto a scrap of paper. Cut out the entire design with an X-Acto knife, leaving a sun-shaped hole in the middle of the paper to create a stencil. Stamp the circle face on scrap paper and cut it out to make a mask (see Masking, page 6).

10 Open the card and lay it flat. Place the sun rays around the opening on the front of the card. Lay the circle face mask over the opening where the face will go. Use a foam sponge to smudge the gold pigment ink onto the card, being careful not to move the stencil.

11 Centered below the sun face on the front, spell out *you* using the alphabet stamps and black dye ink, and *are my sunshine* inside on the folded flap.

12 Stamp the sun in gold pigment ink on the inside of the card just above the word *sunshine*.

Bee Pillow

MATERIALS

Woven cotton fabric, ¾ yard

Pillow form, 14-inch square

Black fabric ink

TooMuchFun bee stamp

The classic simplicity of this crisp, white pillow with its single black bee will make it a favorite for summer lounging.

1 Cut two 20-inch squares of fabric.

2 Stamp the bee in the center of each piece using black fabric ink.

3 Heat set the bee by ironing on the back of each piece after the ink is dry.

4 With right sides together, sew around three sides with white thread, leaving a one-half-inch seam allowance. Turn inside out and press.

5 Insert the pillow form and hand stitch the opening.

6 Using a zipper foot on your sewing machine, topstitch close to the edge of the pillow to create a two-inch border.

Paper Coasters & Take-out Boxes

The bees of summer will be welcome at any picnic when they arrive on these coasters and lunch boxes.

MATERIALS

Blank paper coasters

Kraft take-out boxes

Black permanent craft ink

White and yellow colored pencils

Black fine-tip pen

TooMuchFun bee stamp

Personal Stamp Exchange bee stamp

1 Stamp the large bee in the center of each coaster using black permanent craft ink. Set the ink on each coaster using a heat gun so drippy drinks don't ruin the image.

2 Randomly stamp the small bee in black on the kraft take-out boxes. Allow to dry.

3 Using colored pencils, color the bees' wings white and the bodies yellow.

4 Draw dashed flight lines between bees with a black pen.

Cutaway Tulip Card

Floral Vellum Card with Beads

Floral Fold Note

Pressed Flower Gift Tag

SEPTEMBER

Beautiful flowers are beginning to fade from our gardens,

making this a perfect time to immortalize them in greeting

cards. These lovely floral cards are suitable for sympathy,

wedding, or note cards. The intricate images of the floral

stamps on September's cards rival Mother Nature herself.

Cutaway Tulip Card

MATERIALS

Yellow-green card stock, 7½ by 11 inches

Dark olive-green card stock, 4¼ by 4¼ inches

White chrome-coat card stock, approximately 5 by 5 inches

Black card stock, 3¼ by 3¼ inches

Gold, light purple, dark purple, and lavender brush markers

Magenta tulip stamp

The cutout technique used to create this card may be used with many stamped images to give a dramatic, three-dimensional effect.

1 Score and fold the yellow-green paper to 5½ by 7½ inches.

2 Ink the tulip stamp using the brush markers. Beginning with the stamen, use the gold marker. Then have some fun blending: beginning in the throat of the flower, use the darkest purple marker, then lighter purple, overlapping the light and dark inks and extending toward the outside edges of the petals.

Apply the lavender marker, again overlapping the previous color, and finishing to the edge of the petals. The tips of your markers will pick up a bit of the other colors, but this isn't a problem when it's a similar hue. Breathe heavily on the inked stamp to remoisturize the inks. Stamp in the center of the white chrome-coat paper.

3 Using a paper cutter, trim the image, leaving a one-quarter-inch border.

4 Cut away the white background in the design using an X-ACTO knife.

5 Center and glue the olive-green paper to the black paper, then glue the black to the folded card,

centered horizontally, two inches from the lower edge.

6 Cut four strips of double-stick mounting foam, trim to fit each corner, and tape on the back of the tulip square. Center and mount the square on the black paper.

7 Finish the card by writing or stamping a senti-ment of your choice inside.

Floral Vellum Card with Beads

The layers of this card are held together with tiny seed beads. When you mail the card, protect the beads with a layer of felt or a foam packing sheet and request that it be hand canceled. This card fits in a 5½-inch-square envelope.

MATERIALS

Ivory card stock, 5½ by 11 inches and 4 by 4 inches

Olive-green card stock, 4¾ by 4¾ inches

Lightweight vellum, 5 by 5 inches

Olive-green dye ink

Magenta large floral stamp

Clear, silver-lined glass seed beads, 4

1 Score and fold the large ivory paper to 5½ by 5½ inches.

2 Stamp the large floral design in olive-green in the center of the small ivory square.

3 Center the stamped floral square beneath the vellum square (the design should show through) and hold them together with paper clips.

4 Using a needle and thread, attach the beads by sewing from the back of the ivory card, through the vellum, through the bead, and back through the same hole. Secure the thread ends on the back with adhesive tape. Repeat for each corner.

5 Glue the stamped ivory square to the center of the green paper, then glue the green to the center of the folded ivory card.

Pressed Flower Gift Tag

MATERIALS

*Ivory card stock,
4¼ by 8½ inches*

White pigment ink

White embossing powder

*Rubber Stampede brushed
leaf stamp*

*White or ivory, 3-inch-wide
organdy ribbon,
8 inches long*

Pressed flower

*The delicate pressed
flower suspended in
organdy makes this a
unique tag for a wedding
or shower gift. Press
your fresh flowers in a
traditional flower press,
or in the new type that
dries flowers in the
microwave in mere
seconds.*

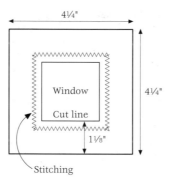

1 Score and fold the ivory paper to make folded card, 4¼ by 4¼ inches

2 On the front of the card, measure and lightly mark the window cutout with a pencil, as shown in the illustration.

3 Cut the window opening using an X-Acto knife and straight edge.

4 Randomly stamp the brushed leaf around the border in white. Heat emboss with white embossing powder.

5 Fold the organdy ribbon in half lengthwise and center it between the card layers, under the window.

6 Gently insert the pressed flower between the ribbon layers. Dab a bit of glue stick behind the flower to hold it in place. Paper clip the layers together.

7 Using a wide, open zigzag stitch on the sewing machine, sew a one-quarter-inch border around the window.

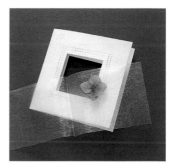

8 Write or stamp *to* and *from* on the back. To tie to a package, punch a hole in one corner and insert a ribbon or cord.

Floral Fold Note

The simple composition of this autumn fold note can be easily changed by experimenting with different paper colors and stamps.

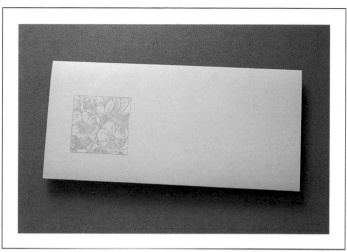

MATERIALS

Light olive-green card stock, 8½ by 10 inches

Lavender card stock, 2¾ by 2¾ inches

Ivory card stock, 3 by 3 inches

Olive-green dye ink

Lavender and purple colored pencils

Magenta floral square stamp

Sticker

1 Stamp the floral square in olive-green in the center of the ivory paper. Using a paper cutter, trim to one-quarter inch from the stamped border. Color the flowers with lavender and purple pencils.

2 Center and glue the stamped ivory paper to the lavender paper.

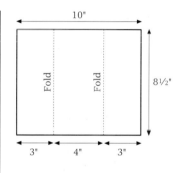

10"

Fold   Fold

8½"

3"   4"   3"

3 Score and fold the olive-green paper as shown in the illustration.

4 Glue the layered, stamped papers one-half inch from the top edge of the green card, centering them horizontally between the folds.

5 Stamp the floral square in olive-green on the outside of the fold note to the left of the mailing address area.

6 After writing your note, secure the folded flap with a sticker.

Trick-or-Treat Pack

Jack-O'-Lantern Photo Card

Halloween Party Invitation

Escaping Ghost Card

OCTOBER

As Halloween approaches and night overtakes the daylight,

our party and greeting card themes turn to ghosts and

witches and things that go bump in the night. There is no

shortage of spirited projects that will celebrate the magical,

eerie fantasies of one of our wildest months.

Trick-or-Treat Pack

MATERIALS

*Shiny white card stock,
2 by 2 inches*

*Dark tan card stock,
8½ by 11 inches*

Black tissue, 1 sheet

Black pigment ink

Clear embossing powder

*Ducks in a Row scaredy
cat stamp*

Impress Happy Haunting
stamp

*Uptown jack-o'-
lantern stamp*

*Orange and yellow
pens*

Pin back, 1 inch

Delight the trick-or-treaters in your life with this fun package. The jack-o'-lantern on the front is a removable pin.

1 Draw the bag pattern shown in the illustration on the dark tan paper.

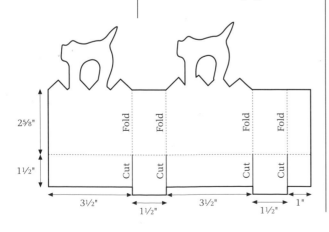

2 Stamp the cat in black and heat emboss with clear embossing powder. Stamp *Happy Haunting* in black.

3 Cut out the package, using an X-Acto knife to cut below the cat's body. Score and fold.

4 Stamp the jack-o'-lantern in black on shiny white paper. Color with orange and yellow pens. Use a laminator to coat both sides with clear plastic (if you

don't have a plastic laminator, you can do this at a commercial copy center). Cut around the jack-o'-lantern close to the outside lines.

5 Attach the jack-o'-lantern to the pin back with double-stick mounting foam. Pierce the lower right side of the package front twice to insert the pin.

6 Apply double-stick adhesive tape to the side extension and form the package by attaching the side extension to the back of the left fence. Fold in the side bottom flaps, then the front and back bottom flaps. Secure with adhesive tape. Insert the black tissue and fill with goodies.

Jack-O'-Lantern Photo Card

A picture of your favorite little ghosts or goblins personalizes this Halloween greeting.

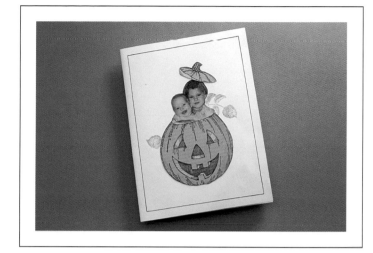

MATERIALS

White chrome-coat card stock, 7 by 10½ inches

Orange card stock, 5 by 4 inches

Black and green pigment inks

Clear embossing powder

Black fine-tip pen

Hero Arts great pumpkin stamp

Remarkables leaf stamp

Impress Trick or Treat stamp

Photograph

1 Score and fold the white paper to 5¼ by 7 inches.

2 Photocopy your photograph, reducing or enlarging it to fit atop the pumpkin opening.

3 Cut around the subjects in the photo and discard the background.

4 Stamp the pumpkin in black on the orange paper. Heat emboss with clear embossing powder.

5 Using an X-ACTO knife, cut out the pumpkin, then cut off the top.

6 Position and glue the photocopy and pumpkin on the front of the card. Glue the pumpkin top above the photo.

7 Stamp the leaf on both sides of the pumpkin in green.

8 Use a black pen and straight edge to draw a border approximately one-quarter inch from the edge.

9 Stamp *Trick or Treat* or a party invitation inside in black.

Halloween Party Invitation

MATERIALS

Black card stock, 5 by 6½ inches

Tan card stock, 4 by 5½ inches

Lightweight vellum, 8½ by 11 inches

Parchment, black, and fawn pigment inks

Clear embossing powder

Black marking pen

Silver fine-tip pen

Imaginations sponged square stamp

Personal Stamp Exchange three witches and moon witch stamps

Imaginations cauldron stamp

This clever postcard hides a party invitation in a secret compartment underneath the bubbling witches' cauldron.

1 Stamp sponged squares in parchment ink along all four edges of the black paper to create a checkered border.

2 Stamp the witches and cauldron in black on the tan paper. Heat emboss both images with clear embossing powder and color the cauldron with the black marking pen.

3 Write (or print on a computer) *We're brewing something up* in black ink.

4 Using a straight edge and rotary cutter with a perforator edge (see Cutting Tools, page 9), cut a perforated line around the sides and bottom of the tan paper.

5 Round off the lower right perforated corner with an X-ACTO knife. On the black paper where it will show through the tan paper's rounded corner, write *lift* in tiny letters in silver.

6 Print the party information on the vellum with a computer printer or rubber stamps. Trim the vellum to 3 by 6 inches.

7 Stamp the moon witch in fawn over the printing on the vellum.

8 Glue the top of the vellum to the upper back of the tan paper. Fold the vellum to fit beneath the perforated opening. (You can also make a long sheet and pleat it to fit.)

9 Glue the tan paper to the black card, applying rubber cement on the outside edges, beyond the perforated line.

10 Use a white or silver pen to write your guest's name and address on the back.

Escaping Ghost Card

The tiny premade envelope on this card provides many creative opportunities. For Halloween, it makes a perfect escape hatch for this whimsical ghost. You can also glue one on a Valentine card, overflowing with hearts, or tie one with a ribbon as a gift tag.

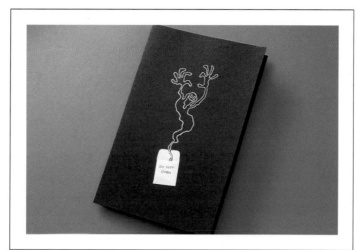

Black card stock, 8½ by 11 inches

White premade envelope, 1-inch square

White pigment ink

White embossing powder

Black fine-tip pen

Stamps by Judith big ghost stamp

Impress Happy Haunting stamp

1 Score and fold the black paper to 5½ by 8½ inches.

2 Stamp the ghost in white 1½ inches from the top of the card. Heat emboss with white embossing powder.

3 Open the card and trim around the bottom three-quarters-inch of the ghost with an X-ACTO knife.

4 Open the flap of the envelope and write *DO NOT OPEN* in black. Slip the ghost's tail over the envelope flap and just inside it. Glue the envelope in place.

5 Stamp *Happy Haunting* inside in white.

Cocktail Party Invitation

Book-Style Invitation

Square Photo Invitation

Explosive New Year's Eve Invitation

November

November's short days and long, crisp nights get me

dreaming of entertaining during the festive holiday season

to come. An invitation sets the mood for any event, and I

especially like to create party invitations that reflect my

personal style. The invitations here can easily be adapted to

fit any special event in your life. When you are producing a

lot of invitations, your computer can be especially useful for

printing party information—particularly if you select a font

that enhances the overall design of the card.

Cocktail Party Invitation

MATERIALS

Silver metallic card stock, 4 by 7 inches

Heavyweight vellum, 8½ by 11 inches (makes 3 invitations)

Black and gold pigment inks

Gold sparkle embossing powder

Hero Arts Press-A-Frame embossing template

Impress you're invited *and martini glass stamps*

Eyelets, 2

Use this martini glass or any rubber stamp of your choosing to tailor an invitation to a particular party theme or to let your guests know just how formal or informal your event will be.

1 Use a computer or an invitation stamp to compose the party information on the vellum as shown in the illustration. If you are using a computer, position the text area horizontally (landscape mode). Three invitations will fit on one piece of vellum.

2 Using a paper cutter, cut the printed vellum sections to 6½ by 3½ inches, centering the text.

3 Using the Press-A-Frame template, pressure emboss the curved square approximately one-half inch from the top edge, centered horizontally. The printed side of the vellum should be facing down so that the embossed image is pressed forward.

4 Turn the vellum over and stamp the martini glass in black in the center of the embossed square. Allow to dry.

5 Stamp *you're invited* in gold, centered between the embossed square and the printed text. Heat emboss with gold sparkle embossing powder.

6 Center the vellum over the silver card. Punch one-eighth-inch holes in the upper corners and affix the metal eyelets.

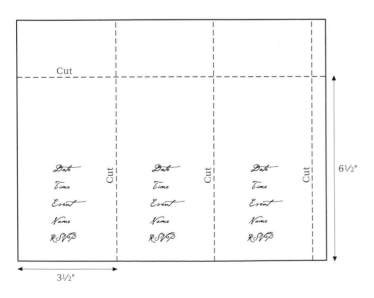

Square Photo Invitation

This invitation was designed for a surprise birthday party for my mother. Because we were inviting people who have known her many years, I set off the invitation with a picture of her in her high school majorette uniform. It was a hit!

MATERIALS

Gold metallic card stock, 5½ by 5½ inches

Lightweight vellum, 4½ by 4½ inches

Ivory card stock, 8½ by 11 inches

Gold metallic pencil

Colorless blender pen

Photocopy of photograph

Premade square envelope

Gold sticker

1 Use a computer or an invitation stamp to compose the party information text on the vellum square. If you're using a computer to compose and print your invitation, you may want to start with 8½-by-11-inch paper, then trim to size.

2 It is tricky to glue vellum to coated paper. Center the vellum over the metallic paper and apply a thin stroke of rubber cement to the gold paper where the top and bottom edges of the vellum will go. Lay the vellum down, then gently lift it so a thin layer of rubber cement is left on the vellum and gold paper. Let this rubber cement dry about twenty to thirty seconds. Now lay it back in place on the gold paper.

3 Print *you're invited* with a computer printer or stamp the words diagonally on the ivory card, below the center. Trim to four by four inches.

4 Transfer the photocopy image with a colorless blender pen onto the ivory card, placing the image diagonally (see Photo Transfer, page 6).

5 Using a straight edge and gold pencil, draw a one-sixteenth-inch border along the edge of the ivory card.

6 Lay the printed ivory card diagonally over the vellum invitation. Enclose both pieces in the premade square folder envelope and seal with a gold sticker.

Book-Style Invitation

MATERIALS

*Ivory card stock,
two 8½-by-11-inch sheets*

*Lightweight vellum,
two 8½-by-11-inch sheets*

*Blue-silver ribbed gift wrap,
5½ by 10 inches*

Silver pigment ink

Dark blue dye ink

Colorless blender pen

*Hot Potatoes number
stamps*

Magenta large clock stamp

Eyelets, 2

Photocopy of portrait

This format includes four pages, but you can include as many pages as you need. One page could be a self-addressed, stamped RSVP card, perforated to pull out and mail. This reunion invitation was personalized with yearbook pictures.

1 For page one, use a computer to print names and addresses as shown in the illustration. Two invitations will fit on one 8½-by-11-inch sheet of ivory paper. Use a paper cutter to trim each page to 5½ by 8½ inches.

2 Lay the photocopy face down to the left of the name and address and transfer the image with a colorless blender pen

(see Photo Transfer, page 6).

3 For the second page, cut one sheet of vellum to 5½ by 8½ inches. Stamp the years—1972 and 1997 in this case—with large number stamps in

silver. Allow to dry. The second year actually runs off the sheet. Stamp the large clock in dark blue, overlapping the second year and running off the sheet.

4 Use a second piece of ivory paper to print the party information on the

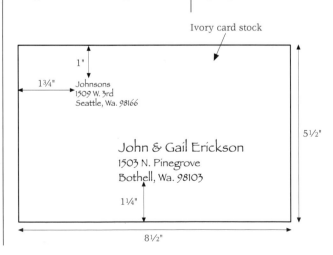

84

computer, again two per sheet. Experiment with font size, italics, and bold print within the text. Cut each page to 5½ by 8½ inches.

5 Use the last sheet of vellum to print a map. Cut to 5½ by 8½ inches.

6 Stack the four pages, face up.

7 Score and fold the gift wrap as shown in the illustration. Insert the collated invitation pages beneath the flap of blue gift wrap on the left.

8 Punch two one-eighth-inch holes through all layers. Affix the eyelets.

9 Close the book with a small (one-half inch) piece of adhesive tape across the open end of the pages.

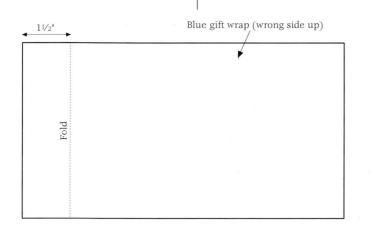

1½"

Fold

Blue gift wrap (wrong side up)

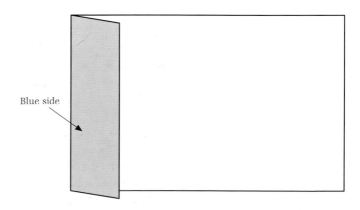

Blue side

Explosive New Year's Eve Invitation

MATERIALS

*Black card stock,
4 by 11 inches*

*Metallic gold card stock,
2¾ by 6¼ inches and
2¾ by 1½ inches*

*Ivory card stock,
3 by 8½ inches*

*Silver and gold pigment
inks*

*Silver sparkle embossing
powder*

Black fine-tip pen

*Mail Expressions
champagne bottle and cork
stamps*

DeNami It's a Party *stamp*

Party cracker snap strip

A party cracker strip hidden behind the champagne bottle makes this invitation open with a bang. The loud crack is similar to a tiny firecracker, so I recommend putting a warning on the label. This card is also fun for any congratulatory event.

1 Stamp the big champagne bottle and cork stopper in silver on ivory paper. Heat emboss with silver sparkle embossing powder. Cut out the bottle just outside the line, trim off the top of the bottle close to the line, and cut off the bottom of the cork stopper. *Note:* If you want to print the card instructions with a computer rather than writing them by hand, do so before you stamp the champagne bottle (see step 7).

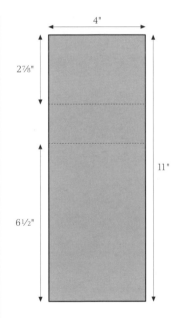

2 Score fold lines on the black paper as shown in the illustration.

3 Stamp *It's a Party* in gold between the fold lines on the black paper.

4 Position the snap joint part of the cracker snap strip beneath the bottle neck. Holding the bottle and snap strip together, position the bottle over the black paper as it will appear in the finished card. Glue the strip to the lower 6½-inch segment only of the black paper, being careful not to put any glue under the snap joint.

5 Glue the large gold paper to the black over the snap strip on the lower part of the card. Align and glue the small gold paper directly to the top of the black paper.

6 Glue the champagne bottle to the gold paper with the lip of the bottle extending just over the top edge. Fold and crease the

black paper. Glue the top of the snap strip to the gold paper at the top of the card. Position and glue the cork over the snap strip. Trim the snap strip end even with the black paper.

7 Using a black pen, write on the front of the bottle, *Grip tabs and pull apart— 1999* (or appropriate year) *—Hold away from face.*

Photo Holiday Greeting Card

Christmas Gift Bag & Tree Ornament

Holiday Paper Mitten

Spiral Christmas Tree Card

Christmas Greeting Card

DECEMBER

Put your creative talents to work for December's long-awaited

holidays. Greeting cards, gift tags, gift wrap, and gifts are all

the more personal when adorned with rubber stamping. The

task is the most fun if you begin your projects before this

hectic month arrives. Any of the cards in this book will take

on a new look when stamped with holiday themes in the

traditional Christmas green and red. The contemporary

projects here present a fresh view of Christmas, which can be

tailored to fit your personal holiday theme.

Photo Holiday Greeting Card

MATERIALS

*Ivory card stock,
4 by 5½ inches*

*Lightweight vellum,
4½ by 6 inches*

*Light green card stock,
5 by 6½ inches*

Silver cord, 15 inches long

*Stampendous ornament
template*

*Photograph—image should
fit in a 2¾-inch-diameter
circle*

*A card that includes a
photograph as part of the
design will make a
personal connection from
you to everyone on your
list. The top two layers of
this card swing out of the
way to reveal a clear
view of the photograph.*

1 Pressure emboss the
ornament template (see
Pressure Embossing, page
6), centered on the ivory
paper.

2 Using the template as a
guide, cut out the ornament
circle with an X-Acto knife.

3 Glue the photo to the
green paper, positioning it
to show through the
ornament opening.

4 Center the vellum over
the green paper and center
the embossed ivory card
over the vellum.

5 Holding all three layers
together, punch a one-
quarter-inch hole through
all layers at the top center.

6 String the silver cord
through the holes and tie.

7 Stamp your Christmas
greeting on the back.

Christmas Gift Bag & Tree Ornament

A handmade gift, like this tree ornament and gift bag, is the most treasured of all. Rubber stamps provide myriad ways to create gifts and personalize their presentation.

MATERIALS

Gift bag

Silvery white glass ball

Tissue paper

White and silver pigment inks

White embossing powder

Silver sparkle embossing powder

Impress Christmas, Magic, holly, and star stamps

Personal Stamp Exchange small solid star stamp

Silver, 3-inch-wide organdy ribbon, 24 inches long

White 1 1/2-inch-wide organdy ribbon, 24 inches long

White 3-inch-wide organdy ribbon, 32 inches long

Gift tag

GIFT BAG

1 To achieve a clear stamped impression on the bag, insert a paperback book inside to provide a firm surface to press the stamp against.

2 Stamp the bag with *Christmas, Magic,* and holly in white and heat emboss with white embossing powder.

3 Tie a bow with the silver and white organdy ribbons and add tissue and a gift tag for a stunning presentation.

CHRISTMAS TREE ORNAMENT

1 Randomly stamp the small stars in silver on a silvery white glass ornament. Sprinkle with silver sparkle embossing

powder. Use pliers to hold the ornament by the cap as you melt the embossing powder with the heat gun.

2 Tie with a white organdy bow for a festive hostess gift or dinner party favor.

Christmas Greeting Card

MATERIALS

Light olive-green card stock, 3³⁄₄ by 8¹⁄₂ inches

Ivory card stock, 3¹⁄₄ by 8¹⁄₄ inches

Lightweight vellum, 7¹⁄₂ by 8¹⁄₂ inches

Silver pigment ink

Light olive-green colored pencil

Green ¹⁄₂-inch-wide ribbon, 12 inches long

Hero Arts Press-A-Frame embossing template

Impress holly, car with Christmas tree, gift package, and Holiday Cheer *stamps*

Eyelet, 1

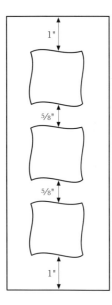

Before this card is even opened, the sheer mailing sleeve and ribbon signal that something special has arrived.

1 Using the Press-A-Frame template, pressure emboss the curvy square three times on the ivory paper as shown in the illustration (see Pressure Embossing, page 6).

2 Stamp in silver on ivory paper, the holly, car with Christmas tree, and package sketches, one in each embossed frame.

3 Color each stamped image with a light olive colored pencil.

4 With the silver pigment ink pad, ink only the word *Holiday* on the Holiday Cheer stamp. Stamp *Holiday* across the top of the ivory paper. Clean the stamp, then ink only *Cheer* and stamp it across the bottom.

5 Score and fold the vellum to make a folded sleeve, 8¹⁄₂ by 3³⁄₄ inches.

6 Lay the ivory paper over the light olive-green paper, aligned at the top and centered. Insert both pieces in the vellum sleeve.

7 Punch a one-eighth-inch hole at the top center through all pieces and install the eyelet.

8 Slip one end of the ribbon through the eyelet and tie a double knot.

9 Write the address and return address on the back of the mailing sleeve.

Holiday Paper Mitten

This round paper mitten makes a great party favor, tree ornament, or place card for your holiday table. Slip a packet of hot cocoa mix and a cookie inside to warm someone's heart.

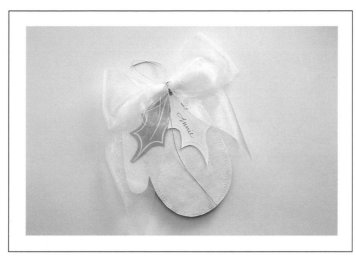

MATERIALS

Ivory gift wrap, 9 by 12 inches

Ivory card stock, 3 by 5 inches

Light green card stock, 3 by 5 inches

Silver tissue, 1 sheet

White pigment ink

Light green and silver pigment ink or pens

White embossing powder

DeNami large holly leaf stamp

Ivory, 3-inch-wide organdy ribbon, 36 inches

Silver cord, 24 inches

Silver eyelet

1 Fold the gift wrap in half with right sides out to make a folded piece, 6 by 12 inches. Hold the loose edges together with paper clips.

2 Draw the mitten pattern shown in the illustration onto the gift wrap.

3 With your sewing machine set on an open, wide zigzag stitch, sew inside the mitten outline using ivory thread. Backstitch at the beginning and end. Leave the top open.

4 Cut just inside the pattern line, being careful not to cut the stitching.

5 Stamp the large holly leaf in white on both the light green and ivory papers. Heat emboss with white embossing powder.

6 Trim about one-quarter inch outside the embossed outline.

7 Write or stamp *To:* in light green on the ivory leaf and *From:* in silver on the green leaf.

8 Lay the base of the ivory leaf over the base of the green leaf. Punch a one-eighth-inch hole through both leaf layers. Punch a hole through the top layer of the mitten.

9 Affix the eyelet through the two holly leaves, from front to back.

10 Insert the silver cord through the eyelet, through the hole in the mitten, and around the ivory ribbon to form a bow. Tie the silver cord in a bow. After inserting a treat, stuff the mitten opening with silver tissue.

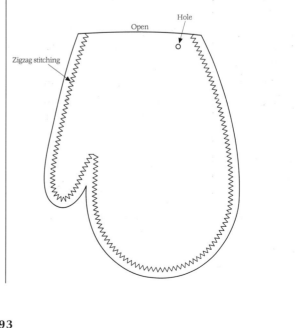

Spiral Christmas Tree Card

MATERIALS

Metallic silver card stock,
7½ by 11 inches

Light green card stock,
4 by 4¼ inches

Ivory card stock,
4 by 4¼ inches

Gold pigment ink

Gold sparkle embossing
powder

Metallic silver colored pencil

Impress large swirl
tree stamp

Impress Joy to the World
stamp

*The center of this
clever spiral-cut tree lifts
to reveal a Christmas
message underneath.*

Cutting line

1 Score and fold the silver
paper to 5½ by 7½ inches.

2 Stamp the large swirl
tree in gold in the center of
the ivory card. Heat emboss
with gold sparkle
embossing powder.

3 Using an X-ACTO knife,
cut just inside the line that
spirals through the tree as
shown in the illustration.

4 Cut a curvy edge along
the ivory paper as shown in
the illustration. Draw a
border with the silver
pencil, following the curved
outline of the ivory paper.
Draw very lightly first, then
fill in with a heavier stroke.

5 Center the stamped tree
over the green paper. Lift
the spiral cutout and lightly
mark with a pencil the
bottom, top, and sides of
the opening.

6 Remove the ivory paper
and stamp *Joy to the World*
in gold within the marks on
the green paper. Heat
emboss with gold sparkle
embossing powder.

7 Apply rubber cement
along the outside edge of
the ivory paper and glue it
to the center of the green
paper. Before pressing in
place, check to see that *Joy
to the World* is visible when
the spiral tree is lifted.

8 Glue the green paper to
the front of the silver card,
centered horizontally and
just above center vertically.

9 Write or stamp a holiday
sentiment inside in silver.

Sources

STAMPS, INK, PAPER, AND SPECIAL PRODUCTS

Impress Rubber Stamps
120 Andover Park East,
  Suite 140,
Tukwila, WA 98166
Phone (206) 901-9101
Fax (206) 901-0221

Rubber Stampede
P.O. Box 246
Berkeley, CA 94701
Phone (800) NEAT-FUN

PAPER AND ENVELOPES

Paper Zone
1915 First Avenue South
Seattle, WA 98134
Phone: (206) 267-1028
Fax (206) 682-4774

BLANK CARDS

Memory Box
Phone: (888) 723-1484

ORDER NUMBERS FOR STAMPS, STENCILS, AND TEMPLATES

All Night Media: cake boy (893E)

Co-Motion: flower pot (1826)

Darcie's Country Folk: solid stripe (K1064)

DeNami: party info (F83), large holly leaf (N32), it's a party (H61)

Dottie's Darlings: flower bouquet (A232), country rose (L114)

Ducks in a Row: scaredy cat (66e)

Fred B. Mullett: salal (093F), salal branch (090H)

Good Stamp: wedding ring (21-51A)

Graven Images: flower pot (447F)

Hero Arts Rubber Stamps: balloon (D1207), great pumpkin (H276), Press-A-Frame, solid heart (A165), swirl (A1294)

Hot Potatoes: large alphabet set (HPUC2), numbers (HPNU2)

Imaginations: sponged square (A344), bouquet (A232), cauldron (F601)

Impress Rubber Stamps: teacup square (4462), heart spiral (4352), rose pot valentine (4410), ribbon heart frame (4411), wavy square frame (4439), large and small swirl roses (4447 and 4453), daisy (4463), three-dot (4448), large leaf (4446), small leaf (4452), citrus full-slice (4457), citrus half-slice (4456), thank you (4468), Trick or Treat (4416), Happy Haunting (4414), you're invited (4503), martini glass (4492), Christmas (4422), magic (4425), holly bough (4419), star (4484), Joy to the World (4434), car with Christmas tree (4495), holly (4494), package (4495), large swirl tree (4424); Holiday Cheer (4517), Congratulations (4551), thank you (4550) Happy Birthday (4549)

Inkadinkadoo: swirl (479I)

Lasting Impressions: flower embossing template, thank you stamp

Leavenworth Jackson: circle face (722F)

Magenta: line heart, large floral (19.097.P), polka dot (18.024.A), small floral square (19.005.I), large clock (29.005.P)

Mail Expressions: champagne bottle (406M), cork (453F)

Marks of Distinction: large angel (HD-63), Sun-Olivia (1157)

Mostly Animals: small baby shoes (912-S5), baby feet (132-S2.2)

Personal Stamp Exchange: flying bee (A608), birdhouse (K2143), star (A262), large crown (F1784), moon witch (E2054), three witches (G1518)

Picture Show: tree (624)

Portfolio: hands and confetti (F337)

Posh Impressions: carrot (Z585E)

Printworks: ribbon set (K1245), sweet on you (C1615)

Remarkables: leaf (no order number)

Renaissance Rubber: Happy Easter (LE498C)

Rubber Stampede: alphabet set (710.01), leaf set (tray collection #700.20), brushed leaf

Rubber Stamps of America: bunny (060), shovel

Stamp Francisco: watering can, large diamond

Stampendous: ornament stencil (ET010)

Stamps by Judith: large package (T-08), ghost (S-19)

TooMuchFun. bee (2018H)

Uptown Rubber Stamps: airmail bird (E13040)

SPECIAL PRODUCTS AVAILABLE FROM IMPRESS RUBBER STAMPS

Alphabet beads

Blank slide frames

Charms, plastic pacifier and silver hearts

Computer fonts

Decorative paper

Double-stick mounting foam

Eyelets and eyelet installation and finishing tools

Heart buttons

Microwave flower press

Paper coasters

Party cracker snap

Pearlescent liquid acrylic

Premade envelopes and gift bags

Ribbon

Ribbon roses

Shipping tags

Take-out boxes

RECOMMENDED READING

Taormina, Grace. 1996. *The Complete Guide to Rubber Stamping*. Lakewood, N.J.: Watson-Guptill Crafts.

Michelle Abel. 1991. *Rubber Stamping, Easy as 1, 2, 3*. Wayzata, Minn.: Creative Press

Bet Borgeson. 1997. *Basic Colored Pencil Techniques*. Cincinnati, Ohio: North Light Books.

Index

accordion fold 23, 62-63
adhesive 8
alphabet bead 44
angel 52

baby shower 45, 47
bag
 trick or treat 74, 76
 baby shower 47
 folded gift bag 38, 47
balance, in design 5
bead 20, 44, 71
bees 60, 62-64, 66-67
binding 10
birdhouse 40
birthday
 book 10
 cards 10, 24, 26-29
 invitations 30, 83
book, for cards 10
book
 invitation format 84
 cover 63
bridal shower 51
brush marker 7, 70
buttons 51

calligraphy 8, 62
Christmas 88-94
coaster 67
color
 selection 5
 ink changes on colored
  paper 7
colored pencil 7
coloring 7
composition 5
computer
 composing text with 54, 84
 fonts 8
congratulations card 17
craft ink 7
cutout
 three-dimensional design 70
 using stencil 90
cutting 9

designing 4-5
die, stamp 5
double-stick tape 8
dye ink 7

Easter 36

embossing 5-7
 heat 17, 27, 40, 51-52, 67,
  76, 78
 pressure 15, 81, 91
eyelet 8, 44, 82, 93

fabric
 book cover 63
 inks 7
 pillow 66
face stamp 64
fasteners 8
Father's Day 53
flowers 15, 35, 68, 70-73
flower press 72
flower ribbon 34
foam tape 8
foam-backed stamp 5
fold, technique 6
fold note 16, 73
fonts, computer 8

ghost 79
gift bag 38, 47, 91
gift tag 40
gift-card packet 59
gluing 8

Halloween 74-79
heart stamp 20
heat embossing 5, 17, 27, 40,
 51-52, 67, 76, 78
heat gun 5
heat-setting inks 7
hole punch 9
holiday
 Christmas 88-94
 Easter 36
 Father's Day 53
 Halloween 74-79
 Mother's Day 46
 New Year's Eve 86
 Valentine's Day 18-24

ink, types 7
invitations
 baby showers 45, 47
 birthdays 32-33, 83
 bridal shower 51
 cocktail party 81
 Halloween party 78
 New Year's Eve party 86
 wedding 54-55

jack-o'-lantern 74, 76-77

keepsake book 10

Le Plume 7
leaf 14
line 5

marker pen 7
Marvy Marker 7
mask 6
masking 6, 22, 50, 64
mitten 93
Mother's Day 46
mounting foam tape 8

New Year's Eve 86
note card 34, 56-58, 70, 73
note card packet 59

ornament, Christmas 90, 91

pad, ink 7
paper 7
paper bag 38
paper cutter 9
party cracker 86
party favor 47
party invitations 32-33, 45, 47,
 53, 78, 81, 83, 86
pens 7
pencils, colored 7
perforation 78
permanent craft ink 7
photo transfers 6, 23, 83-84
photographs 77, 90
picnic box 67
pigment ink 7
pillow 66
place card 93
plastic, ink on 7
powder, embossing 5
press, flower 72
pressure embossing 6, 15, 81, 91
printer, computer 8
proportion 5
pumpkin 75, 76

ribbon, as fastener 8
ribbon rose 34
rotary cutter 9
rubber cement 8
rubber stamps, types of 5

ruler 9

scale 5
scissors, types of 9
scoring 6
self-mailers 16, 73, 84, 92
sewing
 attaching beads 44, 71
 attaching ribbon to card 34
 machine 8, 72
shipping tags 28, 29, 45
showers
 baby 45, 47
 bridal 51
spiral binding 10
spray adhesive 8
stamping, technique 5
stencil 90
stylus, embossing 6
sun 64
supplies 7, 96

take-out box 67
tape 8
techniques 5-6
template, embossing 6
text composition 8
texture 5-7
thank you card 14, 16, 35
thermography 5
Tombow 7
tools 7
tree ornament 90-91
tree stamp 92
trick-or-treat bag 76

valentine 18-24, 50
vellum 7

water-based ink 7
weaving 46
weddings 48-52, 54-55
 cards 50, 52
 invitations 54-55
 showers 53
weight, of papers 7
witch 78
wood-backed stamp 5
wood, inks for 7

X-Acto knife 9